READING *the* BIBLE *through* ADVENT *and* CHRISTMAS

READING *the* BIBLE *through* ADVENT *and* CHRISTMAS

All the daily Advent and Christmas scripture readings from the Catholic liturgy, with guidance for Lectio Divina

Commentaries by ADRIAN GRAFFY

DARTON·LONGMAN+TODD
INTELLIGENT ◆ INSPIRATIONAL ◆ INCLUSIVE
SPIRITUAL BOOKS

This book is dedicated to
Ignatius Suharyo Hardjoatmodjo

First published in Great Britain in 2026 by
Darton, Longman and Todd Ltd
Unit 1, The Exchange
6 Scarbrook Road
Croydon CR0 1UH
editorial@darton-longman-todd.co.uk

This product conforms to the requirements of the European
Union's General Product Safety Regulations (GPSR).
EU Authorised Representative for GPSR:
Easy Access System Europe –
Mustamäe tee 50, 10621 Tallinn, Estonia
gpsr.requests@easproject.com

ISBN: 978-1-917362-36-8

A catalogue record for this book is available from the British Library.

Designed and produced by Judy Linard
Star illustration © Artem @stock.adobe.com

Printed and bound in Great Britain by Bell & Bain, Glasgow

CONTENTS

INTRODUCTION

Welcome to these pages, in which we will reflect on the wonderful collection of Bible readings which we read in the season of Advent. It will come as no surprise, given the Advent theme of the fulfilment of prophecy, that there are many readings from the Hebrew prophets. The Book of Isaiah, with its three sections (1-39, 40-55, and 56-66), features frequently, but several other prophets appear, as well as significant readings from other parts of the Hebrew Scriptures, and related biblical writings. Some of the prophetic readings may be clearly described as 'messianic' since they allude to the coming saviour, but others look to the future in less precise terms.

The responsorial psalms will often echo the themes of the first reading. Their full text is not given here, but care has been taken to ensure that the place of the psalms in the Liturgy of the Word is not disregarded.

The gospel readings in the early days of Advent are chosen to match the first readings from the Hebrew scriptures, and then we have a series of gospels which mention the precursor, John the Baptist. These begin on the Thursday of the second week of Advent and are brought to a close on the Friday of the third week, or on 16th December.

The more intense period of preparation is from 17th December to the morning Mass on 24th December. Advent varies in its length, for Christmas Day may fall on any day (Monday to Sunday) after the Fourth Sunday of Advent. The days omitted will always be those final days of the preparatory period which ends with 16th December.

In the final days of Advent gospel readings from Matthew chapter 1 and Luke chapter 1 are read, so that the stories of events before the birth of Christ and concerning the birth of John the Baptist are presented.

A further important feature is the 'O' antiphons, read from 17th to 23rd December. These *Magnificat* antiphons for Evening Prayer, are also used in the *Alleluia* verses before the gospel of the day. They are given here in their full form, with a brief commentary.

Our Bible translation is the Revised New Jerusalem Bible, edited by Dom Henry Wansbrough, and first published by Darton, Longman and Todd in 2019. It is now published by Hodder & Stoughton. This vibrant translation, in contemporary English, while it retains some elements of traditional biblical parlance, crucially incorporates the insights of modern scholarship. A commentary by Fr Adrian Graffy, appointed to the Pontifical Biblical Commission by Pope Francis in 2014, accompanies each reading.

The Christmas season, which begins with the Vigil Mass for Christmas Day and ends with the Feast of the Baptism of the Lord, offers in the Catholic lectionary an extraordinary richness of biblical readings to accompany and deepen our prayer during this time.

There are four Masses of Christmas Day (the Vigil Mass, the Night Mass, the Dawn Mass and the Day Mass), with three readings each, culminating in the reading of the Prologue of John at the Day Mass.

The octave of Christmas contains the feasts of Stephen, John the Evangelist and the Holy Innocents. The Feast of the Holy Family usually falls on the Sunday in the octave. The octave day itself is the Solemnity of Mary, Mother of God.

Throughout the Christmas season the weekdays allow us to hear passages from the First Letter of John, with its remarkable connections with the Gospel of John. We also continue to read from the infancy narratives of the gospels, which we began to read during Advent, and the whole of John chapter 1. The length of the season varies, which means some of the weekdays will be omitted.

The Solemnity of the Epiphany falls on 6th January, unless for pastoral seasons it is celebrated on a Sunday. Selected gospel passages are read between Epiphany and the Baptism of the Lord, which usually falls on the final Sunday.

As with the previously published *Reading the Bible Through Lent*, the Bible translation used is the Revised New Jerusalem Bible, edited by Dom Henry Wansbrough, and first published by Darton, Longman and Todd in 2019. It is now published by Hodder & Stoughton. This vibrant translation, in contemporary English, while it retains elements of biblical parlance, is not constrained by translations of earlier times, and crucially incorporates insights of modern scholarship. A commentary by Fr Adrian Graffy, member of the Pontifical Biblical Commission since 2014, accompanies each reading.

ADVENT READINGS

FIRST SUNDAY OF ADVENT – YEAR A

A reading from the prophet Isaiah (2:1-5)

The vision of Isaiah son of Amoz, concerning Judah and Jerusalem.
It will happen in the last days
that the mountain of the house of the Lord
will be established as the head of the mountains
and will be lifted above the heights.
Then all the nations will stream to it,
many peoples will come to it and say,
'Come, let us go up to the mountain of the Lord,
to the house of the God of Jacob,
that he may teach us his ways and we may walk in his paths.'
For the Law will come from Zion
and the Word of the Lord from Jerusalem.
Then he will judge between the nations
and arbitrate between many peoples.
They will hammer their swords into ploughshares
and their spears into sickles.
Nation will not lift sword against nation;
no longer will they learn to make war.
House of Jacob, come, let us walk in the light of the Lord.

ADVENT BEGINS WITH Isaiah's vision of peace. His vision is the 'word' (*dabar*) which Isaiah 'saw' (*hazah*) about Judah and Jerusalem. Hearing and seeing are crucial in this prophetic book (Isaiah 6). The focus is on Sion, the mountain of the house of the Lord, towards which the nations stream. There is a universal desire to be taught the 'ways' and the 'paths' of God. Sion, Jerusalem, is the channel by which the Law (*torah*) and the Word (*dabar*) are given. At God's judgement the weapons of war are put to peaceful use, and the whole 'house of Jacob', joined by the nations, walks in the light of the Lord.

Psalm 122 (121) Once again people are making their way to God's house. They go to praise the Lord and to pray for peace, peace for Jerusalem and peace for the brothers and sisters.

A reading from the letter of St Paul to the Romans (13:11-14)

Besides, you know the time has come; now is the moment for you to stop sleeping and wake up, for now our salvation is nearer than when we first began to believe. The night is far gone, day is near; so let us throw off the works of darkness and put on the armour of light. Let us live decently, as in the light of day, not with orgies or drunkenness, promiscuity or licentiousness, not with quarrelling and jealousy. Rather, put on the Lord Jesus Christ, and make no provision for the flesh to fulfil its desires.

ST PAUL TELLS us the 'time' (*kairos*) has come, the hour to arise from sleep, for the longed-for salvation is near at hand. The night is gone, and the 'day' (*hemera*) is approaching, the day of the Lord. He echoes the words of Isaiah, that we should walk 'in the light of the Lord'. Twice he speaks of putting on new clothing: take off the 'works of darkness', and 'put on the armour of light', for Christians are engaged in a battle against the forces of evil. Avoid all that is contrary to Christian life, and 'put on the Lord Jesus Christ'.

A reading from the holy gospel according to Matthew (24:37-44)

Jesus said: 'As it was in Noah's day, so will be the coming of the Son of man. For in those days before the Flood people were eating, drinking, taking wives, taking husbands, until the day Noah went into the ark, and they suspected nothing till the Flood came and swept them all away. So will be the coming of the Son of man. Then of two men in the fields, one is taken, one left; of two women grinding at the mill, one is taken, one left. So stay awake, because you do not know the day when your master is coming.

You may be sure of this, that if the householder had known at what time of the night the burglar would come, he would have stayed awake and would not have allowed anyone to break through the wall of his house. Therefore, you too must stand ready, because the Son of man is coming at an hour you do not expect.'

THE EARLY DAYS of Advent invite us to reflect on the 'second coming', and on our lack of readiness. Jesus speaks about the 'coming' (*parousia*) of the Son of man, the prelude to the end. He insists that the time is not known, but stresses the danger of not being prepared. Noah's contemporaries were unprepared and the flood destroyed them. The destruction is indiscriminate. But the disciples of the Lord are to be prepared, to 'watch', to 'stay awake'. A further parable, about the burglar who breaks into a house, underlines the danger of being unprepared. Jesus repeats the warning to be ready (*hetoimos*) at any hour.

How does reflection on the second coming fit with preparation for the birth of Christ?
Pray for the ability to live in readiness and confidence.

FIRST SUNDAY OF ADVENT – YEAR B

A reading from the prophet Isaiah (63:16b-17,19b; 64:3-7)

You, Lord, are our Father,
'Our Redeemer' is your name from of old.
Why, Lord, do you let us stray from your paths
and harden our hearts so that we do not fear you?
Come back, for the sake of your servants,
the tribes of your heritage.
Oh, that you would tear the heavens open
and come down!
In your presence the mountains would quake.
No ear has heard,
no eye has seen any god but you,
so act like this for those who await him.

You come to meet those who act justly;
by their ways they remember you.
See, you have been angry and we have sinned;
now we persist in your ways and we shall be saved.
We have all been like a thing unclean,
all our righteous deeds like filthy rags.
Like a leaf we, all of us, wither,
and our misdeeds bear us off like the wind.
No one calls on your name,
or attempts to hold fast to you,
for you have hidden your face from us
and given us up to the power of our misdeeds.
And yet, Lord, you are our Father;
we are the clay and you shape us,
all of us are the work of your hands.

THIS PSALM-LIKE READING begins and ends acclaiming God as 'our Father' (*'abinu*). These last chapters of the book of Isaiah date from after the return from the Babylonian exile. God is the 'redeemer' who has freed the people. Once again, they urge him to intervene, to 'tear the heavens open', to show that God is there for the people. Profound awareness of sin leads those who pray to describe themselves as 'unclean', as 'filthy rags', as withered leaves. The return home to the land of Israel has not solved their problems, but they acknowledge their guilt, and know themselves to be clay shaped by the potter. 'We are all of us the work of your hand.'

Psalm 80 (79) The psalm repeatedly calls to God: 'Bring us back.' Using different images the 'shepherd of Israel' is urged to 'visit this vine' and to give life to those who ask for help.

A reading from the first letter of St Paul to the Corinthians (1:3-9)

Grace to you and peace from God our Father and the Lord Jesus Christ. I am continually thanking God about you, for the grace of God given to you in Christ Jesus; for in every way you have been richly endowed in him, in every kind of speech and knowledge, just as the testimony of Christ has been strengthened in you, so that you are not lacking in any gift as you wait for our Lord Jesus Christ to be revealed; he will continue to give you strength till the end, to be irreproachable on the day of our Lord Jesus Christ. God is trustworthy; through him you were called into fellowship with his Son Jesus Christ our Lord.

IN THESE EARLY verses of his first letter to the Corinthians Paul celebrates their faith. Before embarking on criticisms of the community he acknowledges the grace they have received 'in Christ Jesus'. They have been enriched 'in every kind of speech and knowledge'. The 'testimony (*martyrion*) of Christ' has grown among them. Paul emphasises that the Christian community is waiting for the 'revelation' (*apokalypsis*) of our Lord Jesus Christ, and must be prepared for his coming. Finally, God is 'trustworthy' (*pistos*), and it is by God's will that they were called into communion (*koinonia*) with Christ.

A reading from the holy gospel according to Mark (13:33-37)

Jesus said to his disciples: 'Take care, stay awake, because you never know when the time will come. It is like a man travelling abroad, leaving his home, and putting his servants in charge, each with his own work to do; and he has told the doorkeeper to stay awake. So stay awake, because you do not know when the master of the house is coming, evening, midnight, cockcrow or dawn; when he comes unexpectedly, he must not find you asleep. And what I say to you I say to all: Stay awake!'

THESE ARE THE final words of Jesus' discourse on the end of the world. They are punctuated with the call to 'stay awake', familiar in our Advent liturgy. This speaks of the need to live, not in lazy indifference, but responsibly in the present, not gazing aimlessly into the future. Lack of knowledge of the 'time' (*kairos*) makes vigilance even more urgent. The parable of the absent master does not need to be taken to a conclusion. Its meaning is obvious.

What might 'staying awake' mean in your life?
Pray for faith amid the troubles of the world.

FIRST SUNDAY OF ADVENT – YEAR C

A reading from the prophet Jeremiah (33:14-16)

'Look, the days are coming – declares the Lord – when I shall fulfil the promise of happiness I made to the House of Israel and the House of Judah:
In those days and at that time,
I shall make a righteous Branch grow for David
who will do what is just and righteous in the land.
In those days Judah will triumph
and Jerusalem live in safety.
And this is the name the city will be called:
The-Lord-is-our-Saving-Justice.'

THE PROPHET JEREMIAH announces that God will fulfil the 'promise of happiness', the 'good word' (*dabar tob*), he had spoken. Jeremiah tells of a 'Branch' (*tsemah*), an appropriate living symbol of a righteous ruler from the stock, the line, of David. 'Justice' (*mishpat*) and 'righteousness' (*tsedaqah*) are constantly associated with the desired ruler. The rebuilt kingdom of Judah and its capital, Jerusalem, destroyed by the Babylonians, will be re-established. The name of the final king of Judah, Zedekiah, meant 'the Lord is my justice', but he had failed to live out that justice and had rejected the word of the prophet. The 'saving justice' (*tsedeq*) of God will be found in days to come in the life of the city, rebuilt and renewed.

Psalm 25 (24) The psalm too speaks of the true ways of the Lord, which are proclaimed as 'faithfulness' and 'love'.

A reading from the first letter of St Paul to the Thessalonians (3:12-4:2)

May the Lord fill you to overflowing with love for each other and for all, just as our love for you overflows. And may he so confirm your hearts in holiness that you may be blameless in the sight of our

God and Father at the coming of our Lord Jesus with all his saints.

Finally, brothers and sisters, we urge you and appeal to you in the Lord Jesus that, as we instructed you how to live in the way that pleases God, so you should also live so as to make more progress still. You know what instructions we gave you on the authority of the Lord Jesus.

PAUL SPEAKS OF an overflowing of love (*agape*) between Christians and beyond the Christian family, and of his love for the Christians of Thessalonika. This is coupled with the holiness (*hagiosyne*) which comes from a blameless life. In this way Christians should prepare for the coming (*parousia*) of the Lord 'with all his saints'. The teaching of Paul, given with the authority of the Lord Jesus, is to be the guide in making more and more progress in the life of faith.

A reading from the holy gospel according to Luke (21:25-28, 34-36)

Jesus said to his disciples: 'There will be signs in the sun and moon and stars; on earth distress among nations in confusion at the roaring of the sea and waves, as people faint from fear and expectation of what is coming upon the world, for the powers of the heavens will be shaken. And then they will see the *Son of man coming in a cloud* with power and great glory. When these things begin to take place, stand erect, hold your heads high, because your liberation is drawing near.

'Watch yourselves, so that your hearts are not weighed down by debauchery and drunkenness and the cares of life, and that day comes upon you unexpectedly, like a trap. For it will come upon all those living on the face of the whole earth. Stay awake, praying at all times that you may have the strength to escape all these things that are going to happen, and to take your stand before the Son of man.'

THESE LINES ARE from the concluding words of Jesus' discourse about the future and the end. He has spoken of the destruction of Jerusalem, and now speaks of terrifying cosmic events, distress and confusion among the nations. This is the prelude to the high point of these events, the return of the Son of man, coming on the clouds (Daniel 7:13). At this point Christians should 'stand erect' and 'hold their heads high', for this is the moment of 'liberation' (*apolutrosis*). The final words are another encouragement to stay awake, lest the day springs on them 'like a trap', and, crucially in Luke's gospel, to 'pray at all times', as they wait for the coming of the Lord.

How does faith help us amid the dire fears facing humanity?
Pray for the courage to prefer the words of Jesus to the temptations of the world.

MONDAY OF THE FIRST WEEK IN ADVENT

A reading from the prophet Isaiah (2:1-5)

The vision of Isaiah son of Amoz, concerning Judah and Jerusalem.
It will happen in the last days
that the mountain of the house of the Lord
will be established as the head of the mountains
and will be lifted above the heights.
Then all the nations will stream to it,
many peoples will come to it and say,
'Come, let us go up to the mountain of the Lord,
to the house of the God of Jacob,
that he may teach us his ways and we may walk in his paths.'
For the Law will come from Zion
and the Word of the Lord from Jerusalem.
Then he will judge between the nations
and arbitrate between many peoples.
They will hammer their swords into ploughshares
and their spears into sickles.
Nation will not lift sword against nation;
no longer will they learn to make war.
House of Jacob, come, let us walk in the light of the Lord.

THIS READING ANNOUNCES movement in two directions. All the nations will go up to Sion, the mountain of God, and to the 'house' (*bayit*) of the Lord. The house is the temple in Jerusalem where the God of all creation and of all peoples has set his dwelling place. It is the dream of the prophet that God will be recognised beyond the people first chosen so that the men, women and children of the world will flock to God's house. Then there is the movement of the Law, the teaching (*torah*) coming from God, coming out from God's dwelling place. The Word (*dabar*) of God too will come down to teach and feed God's people. The result is peace, for people will reject the ways of war and transform their weapons, their swords and spears, into ploughshares and sickles, to tend and cultivate the earth. In this way God provides 'light' for the peoples of the world.

FIRST READING ON MONDAY IN YEAR A

A reading from the prophet Isaiah (4:2-6)

That day, the Lord's seedling shall be beauty and glory,
the fruit of the land shall be the pride and ornament
of Israel's survivors.
Those who are left in Zion and remain in Jerusalem
will be called holy,
all those in Jerusalem marked out for life.
When the Lord has washed away the filth of Zion's daughters
and, with the wind of judgement and the wind of burning, cleansed
Jerusalem of the blood shed in her,
the Lord will create, over every dwelling on Mount Zion
and over its places of assembly,
a cloud by day and by night smoke with the brightness of a flaring fire.
For over all the glory will be a canopy
and a tent to give shade by day from the heat,
and refuge and shelter from the storm and the rain.

THE PROPHET USES botanical imagery, speaking of the 'seedling' (*tsemah*) of the Lord and the 'fruit of the land', quite possibly to evoke the messianic figure who will rule the 'survivors', the remnant of the people. These will be God's 'holy people' who are 'marked out for life'. Once they have been purged in suffering they will be protected by the Exodus symbols of cloud by day, and fire by night (Ex 13:21), newly 'created' by the Lord. The Lord's glory, in the holy city, will be a 'canopy' and a 'tent' to shield from the heat, and a 'refuge' and 'shelter' to protect from the storm and the rain. God continues to keep the people safe.

Psalm 122 (121) The psalm echoes the reading from Isaiah 2 with the multitudes coming to the temple of the Lord, and the longing for peace. As in both readings from Isaiah, the focus is on the holy city of Jerusalem.

A reading from the holy gospel according to Matthew (8:5-11)

When he went into Capernaum a centurion came up and pleaded with him, saying, 'Lord, my servant is lying at home paralysed and in terrible pain.' Jesus said to him, 'I will come myself and cure him.' The centurion replied, 'Lord, I am not worthy that you should come under my roof; just give the word and my servant will be cured. For I am under authority myself and have soldiers under me; and I say to one man, "Go," and he goes; to another, "Come," and he comes; to my servant, "Do this," and he does it.' When Jesus heard this he was astonished and said to those following him, 'Amen I say to you, in no one in Israel have I found faith as great as this. And I tell you that many will come from east and west and sit down with Abraham and Isaac and Jacob at the feast in the kingdom of Heaven.'

IT IS THEIR faith which brings people 'from east and west' to take their places at the feast of the kingdom. It is faith that has brought the pagan centurion to Jesus, pleading for his paralysed servant, who is in great pain. His faith leads him to trust that, despite Jesus' willingness to visit him, Jesus does not need to go to the servant but can heal simply by speaking a word of command. That the centurion is not a member of the chosen people leads Jesus to be 'astonished' at his faith. It is right to see the connection between the 'many peoples' in Isaiah 2 and those 'from east and west' in the words of Jesus here.

Does my vision of the Church erect boundaries between people, or remove them?

Pray for a deepening sense of gratitude for the universal Church.

TUESDAY OF THE FIRST WEEK IN ADVENT

A reading from the prophet Isaiah (11:1-10)

A branch will spring from the stock of Jesse,
a shoot will grow from his roots.
On him will rest the spirit of the Lord,
the spirit of wisdom and insight,
the spirit of counsel and power,
the spirit of knowledge and fear of the Lord:
his delight will be in fear of the Lord.
His judgement will not be by appearances,
his verdict not given on hearsay.
He will judge the weak with righteousness
and give fair sentence for the poor of the land.
He will strike the violent with the rod of his mouth
and with the breath of his lips bring death to the wicked.
Righteousness will be the belt around his waist
and truth the belt about his hips.
The wolf will live with the lamb,
the leopard lie down with the kid,
calf, lion and fat-stock beast together,
with a little boy to lead them.
The cow and the bear will graze,
their young will lie down together.
The lion will eat hay like the ox.
The infant will play over the hole of the adder,
the baby will put its hand into the viper's lair.
No hurt, no harm will be done on all my holy mountain,
for the land will be full of knowledge of the Lord,
as the waters cover the sea.
That day, the root of Jesse,
standing as a signal for the peoples,
will be sought out by the nations
and its dwelling will be glorious.

THIS IS ONE of just two messianic poems in the first part of Isaiah, the other being found in chapter 9. A branch, a shoot, will spring from the stock of Jesse, father of David. The Spirit of the Lord will rest on him, bestowing six qualities, from 'wisdom' to 'the fear of the Lord'. His role is to judge the weak with righteousness and to rule for the poor with justice, for justice *(tsedeq)* will be his belt, and faithfulness *('emunah)* will be around his waist. Cosmic harmony will be the result, with peaceful relationships established between all living things, as the conditions of paradise return. The vision of Isaiah embraces both justice and the environment, for the land will be full of the 'knowledge of the Lord', a seventh quality of the messianic age. The 'root' of Jesse will be a 'signal', sought after by all peoples, for it reveals the 'glory' (*kabod*) of the Lord to the nations.

Psalm 72 (71), a messianic psalm, reflects the thought of Isaiah 11, presenting the Messiah as bringer of justice, and friend of the poor.

A reading from the holy gospel according to Luke (10:21-24)

Just at this time, filled with joy by the Holy Spirit, Jesus said, 'I bless you, Father, Lord of heaven and of earth, for hiding these things from the learned and the clever and revealing them to little children. Yes, Father, for that was your good pleasure. Everything has been handed over to me by my Father; and no one knows who the Son is except the Father, and who the Father is except the Son and anyone to whom the Son chooses to reveal him.' Then turning to his disciples he spoke to them on their own, 'Blessed are the eyes that see what you see, for I tell you that many prophets and kings wanted to see what you see, and did not see it; to hear what you hear, and did not hear it.'

JESUS IS THE Messiah 'filled with joy by the Holy Spirit' and Jesus prays in thanksgiving to the Father. He says that 'these things' are hidden from the learned and the clever, and revealed to children. The following words of Jesus explain that it is through him that the little ones can know the Father. They are those chosen by Jesus to receive the revelation of the Father. Jesus then identifies some of these 'little ones', by pronouncing his disciples 'blessed' (*makarioi*). They are seeing and hearing the Messiah, long awaited by 'prophets and kings', by both religious and secular leadership.

What do we most treasure in God's revelation?
Pray for a humble heart to be ready to learn new things about God.

WEDNESDAY OF THE FIRST WEEK IN ADVENT

A reading from the prophet Isaiah (25:6-10a)

On this mountain, the Lord Sabaoth is preparing for all peoples
a banquet of rich food, a banquet of fine wines,
of succulent food, of well-strained wines.
On this mountain, he has destroyed
the veil which veiled all peoples,
the pall enveloping all nations.
He has destroyed death for ever.
Lord God has wiped away the tears from every cheek;
he has taken his people's shame away over all the earth,
for the Lord has spoken.
And on that day it will be said,
'Look, this is our God,
in him we put our hope that he would save us.
This is the Lord, we waited for him.
Let us exult and rejoice in his salvation.'
For the Lord's hand will rest on this mountain.

THE 'APOCALYPSE' OF Isaiah in chapters 24-27 points to the future and the end. 'On this mountain', surely Sion, God prepares an exquisite feast for all nations. 'On this mountain', God will remove the veil over people's eyes, they will receive their sight, and God will destroy death for ever. God removes the tears of sadness, and the shame of guilt. This banquet symbolises not superficial and transient gifts but the complete healing offered by God. The people recognise in song the gift of salvation, and the presence of 'the Lord's hand ... on this mountain'. Salvation, not judgement, is God's last word.

> **Psalm 23 (22)** What Isaiah promised to the peoples is received in this psalm by the individual at prayer. The shepherd God prepares a banquet, and welcomes people into the house of God.

A reading from the holy gospel according to Matthew (15:29-37)

Jesus went on from there and reached the shores of the Lake of Galilee, and he went up onto the mountain. He took his seat, and large crowds came to him bringing the lame, the crippled, the blind, the deaf and many others; these they put down at his feet, and he cured them. The crowds were astonished to see the deaf speaking, the crippled whole again, the lame walking and the blind seeing, and they praised the God of Israel.

But Jesus called his disciples to him and said, 'I feel sorry for all these people; they have been with me for three days now and have nothing to eat. I do not want to send them off hungry, or they might collapse on the way.' The disciples said to him, 'Where in a deserted place could we get sufficient bread for such a large crowd to have enough to eat?' Jesus said to them, 'How many loaves have you?' They said, 'Seven, and a few small fish.' Then he instructed the crowd to sit down on the ground, and he took the seven loaves and the fish, and after giving thanks he broke them and began handing them to the disciples, who gave them to the crowds. They all ate as much as they wanted, and they collected what was left of the scraps, seven baskets full.

IN THIS SECOND account of the multiplication of loaves in the Gospel of Matthew Jesus, like God in the Isaiah reading, gives gifts on the mountain. The gifts of healing come first, for the lame, the crippled, the blind and the deaf, and 'many others'. As in the first reading, the people 'praise the God of Israel'. To prepare something for the people to eat Jesus relies on the assistance of the disciples. Though hesitant at first, they bring what they have. As at the Last Supper he will celebrate with them, Jesus gives thanks and breaks the bread. It is the disciples who bring the food to the crowds. Jesus uses the seeds of goodness in their hearts so that even among so many people an abundant amount of food remains.

What challenge does the gospel reading present?
Pray for confidence that God never refuses the gifts we need.

THURSDAY OF THE FIRST WEEK IN ADVENT

A reading from the prophet Isaiah (26:1-6)

That day, this song will be sung in Judah:
'Ours is a strong city.
He has set up the salvation of walls and ramparts.
Open the gates, that the righteous people may come in,
a people that keeps faith!
Those of trustful mind you keep in peace,
in peace because they trust in you.
Trust in the Lord for ever,
for the Lord is a rock of ages.
He has brought low the dwellers on the heights,
the lofty citadel he lays low,
brings it to the ground, flings it down in the dust.
It will be trodden under foot,
by the feet of the oppressed, the steps of the poor.'

A CONTRAST BETWEEN a 'strong city', where the faithful people dwell, and a 'lofty citadel', where others live 'on the heights', lies at the heart of this song to be sung in Judah. The people of the city are 'righteous' (*tsaddiq*). They 'keep faith', they are 'of trustful mind'. These are the virtues which lead to peace (*shalom*). The Lord is described as a 'rock of ages', on whom the people can rely. By contrast those who dwell 'on the heights', in their 'lofty citadel', are brought to the ground, flung into the dust, to be trodden under foot by the very people they have oppressed, and 'by the steps of the poor'. This passage extols faith, and condemns human pride.

Psalm 118 (117) As the righteous entered the city in the Isaiah reading, so the just enter the Lord's 'own gate' in this momentous psalm of the temple liturgy.

A reading from the holy gospel according to Matthew (7:21, 24-27)

Jesus said to his disciples: 'Not everyone who says to me, "Lord, Lord," will enter the kingdom of Heaven, only the person who does the will of my Father in heaven. Therefore, everyone who hears these words of mine and acts on them will be like a sensible person who built a house on rock. Rain came down, floods rose, gales blew and hurled themselves against that house, and it did not fall: it was founded on rock. But everyone who hears these words of mine and does not act on them will be like a stupid person who built a house on sand. Rain came down, floods rose, gales blew and struck that house, and it fell; and what a fall it had!'

ONCE AGAIN WE have a contrast between two buildings, and an emphasis on faith, all in the context of 'entering' the kingdom of heaven. To hear the words of Jesus and to act on them is to build one's house on rock. Whatever is thrown against this house does not bring it down. While the contrast in the first reading was between the faithful righteous people and the proud dwellers on the heights, the contrast here is between those who have the wisdom to heed the words of Jesus, and those who fail to do so. These are the final words of the Sermon on the Mount, inviting all disciples to 'do the will' of the Father by putting into practice the better justice (5:20) preached by Jesus.

How strong is my building of faith?
Pray for clarity and commitment.

FRIDAY OF THE FIRST WEEK IN ADVENT

A reading from the prophet Isaiah (29:17-24)

In just a little while will not Lebanon become fertile land,
and fertile land be taken for a forest?
That day the deaf will hear the words of the book
and, free from shadow and darkness,
the eyes of the blind will see.
The lowly will once more find joy in the Lord
and the poorest of people will delight
in the Holy One of Israel;
for the oppressor will be no more,
the scoffer will have vanished
and all those alert to do evil destroyed –
those who cause people to sin by a word
and those who lay traps for the arbitrator at the gate
and pervert the cause of the righteous.
Therefore, thus says the Lord,
God of the House of Jacob, Abraham's redeemer,
'No more shall Jacob be ashamed,
no more shall his face grow pale,
for when his children see the work of my hands in their midst
they will hallow my name,
they will hallow the Holy One of Jacob
and will hold the God of Israel in awe.
The perverted in spirit will learn understanding
and murmurers accept instruction.'

CHANGES IN THE natural world herald changes in people's hearts. Just as fertility increases in Lebanon, so, in a reversal of Isaiah's call vision in chapter 6, the deaf will finally begin to hear, and the blind will begin to see. But it will be the lowly and the poorest who will once again delight in the Lord, for their hearts have always been open to God. This opening up to God's word will come because the 'scoffer' who belittles faith, the 'oppressor' who harms God's people, and those who pervert others are brought to nothing. This vision announces the way of salvation, in which the humble are the first to see God's truth. Then comes a solemnly introduced word of God, that the shame of Jacob is ended, for they see what God's hand can do, and hallow the name of the Holy One of Israel.

Psalm 27 (26) The psalmist also rejoices in God's light, trusting in the full vision of the goodness of the Lord 'in the land of the living'.

A reading from the holy gospel according to Matthew (9:27-31)

As Jesus went on from there two blind men followed him crying out, 'Have mercy on us, son of David.' And when Jesus reached the house the blind men came up to him and he said to them, 'Do you believe I can do this?' They said, 'Yes, Lord.' Then he touched their eyes saying, 'According to your faith, let it be done to you.' And their eyes were opened. Then Jesus sternly warned them, 'Take care that no one knows about this.' But when they had gone away, they talked about him all over the countryside.

ONCE MORE ON this first Friday of Advent it is a question of the blind being able to see. These two blind men already have faith, for they herald Jesus as 'son of David', but Jesus questions them further. It is by touch that he heals their eyes, saying 'according to your faith, let it be done to you'. They are forbidden to speak about the cure, for Jesus is cautious about unwanted popularity and acclaim. But the two formerly blind men, who had enthusiastically proclaimed him 'son of David', are not going to be silenced.

How much sight do you have, how much do you need?
Pray for a new vision of faith, which is not rigid and is willing to grow.

SATURDAY OF THE FIRST WEEK IN ADVENT

A reading from the prophet Isaiah (30:19-21,23-26)

People of Zion dwelling in Jerusalem,
you shall weep no more.
He will be merciful to you when you cry for help;
when he hears it, he will answer you.
Though the Lord has given you
the bread of suffering and the water of distress,
he who is your teacher will no longer remain hidden
and your eyes will see your teacher.
Whether you turn to the right or left
your ears will hear these words behind you,
'This is the way, keep to it.'
He will send rain for the seed you sow in the ground,
and the bread that the ground provides
will be rich and abundant.
On that day, your cattle will graze in wide pastures.
Oxen and donkeys that work the land
will eat wild sorrel for fodder,
winnowed by the shovel and pitchfork.
On every lofty mountain,
on every high hill, there will be streams flowing with water
on the day of the great slaughter when the strongholds fall.
Then moonlight will be bright as sunlight
and sunlight itself be seven times brighter –
like the light of seven days in one –
on the day the Lord dresses the wound of his people
and heals the scars of the blows they have received.

MULTIPLE TRANSFORMATIONS ARE announced in this reading. Transformation from weeping to rejoicing, from suffering and distress to a vision of the true 'teacher', who reassures the people with the words: 'This is the way.' Transformation in nature too with regular rain for the ground, so that the fields are productive, rich bread is plentiful, and good fodder available for animals. The reference to 'streams flowing with water' is coupled with mention of 'the great slaughter when the strongholds fall', for this people, who have known the violence of oppression and war, will see the mighty cast down. The next image is even more majestic as moonlight is 'bright as sunlight' and the sun shines 'seven times brighter'. The Lord, the healer of bodies and hearts, is evoked once more in the final verse of this extraordinary litany of God's works of goodness for the people.

> **Psalm 147 (146)** praises with exuberance the same Lord who 'heals the broken-hearted' and 'binds up their wounds', the same Lord who calls the stars by name.

A reading from the holy gospel according to Matthew (9:35-10:1,6-8)

Jesus made a tour through all the towns and villages, teaching in their synagogues, proclaiming the good news of the kingdom and curing all kinds of disease and all kinds of illness. And when he saw the crowds he felt sorry for them because they were harassed and dejected, like sheep without a shepherd. Then he said to his disciples, 'The harvest is rich but the labourers are few, so ask the Lord of the harvest to send out labourers to his harvest.'

He summoned his twelve disciples and gave them authority over unclean spirits, with power to drive them out and to cure every disease and every illness: 'Go to the lost sheep of the House of Israel. And as you go, proclaim that the kingdom of Heaven is close at hand. Cure the sick, raise the dead, cleanse the lepers, drive out demons. You received without charge, give without charge.'

THE GIFTS OF God in the Isaiah reading are brought by Jesus too: he brings true teaching in their synagogues, he proclaims the good news, and he heals. Like the God of Isaiah, who 'dresses the wound of the people', and the God invoked by the psalmist, who 'heals the broken-hearted', Jesus shows compassion for the 'lost sheep of the house of Israel'. Furthermore, he enlists the help of the Twelve both in proclaiming the Kingdom and in healing. The free gifts they have received are to be given away freely, and in the first place, before the gentile mission, to the people of Israel. The Risen Jesus will send forth his disciples 'to all nations' (Matthew 28).

Why does Jesus send the Twelve to the House of Israel?
Pray for true compassion for Jew and Gentile alike.

SECOND SUNDAY OF ADVENT – YEAR A

A reading from the prophet Isaiah (11:1-10)

A branch will spring from the stock of Jesse,
a shoot will grow from his roots.
On him will rest the spirit of the Lord,
the spirit of wisdom and insight,
the spirit of counsel and power,
the spirit of knowledge and fear of the Lord:
his delight will be in fear of the Lord.
His judgement will not be by appearances,
his verdict not given on hearsay.
He will judge the weak with righteousness
and give fair sentence for the poor of the land.
He will strike the violent with the rod of his mouth
and with the breath of his lips bring death to the wicked.
Righteousness will be the belt around his waist
and truth the belt about his hips.
The wolf will live with the lamb,
the leopard lie down with the kid,
calf, lion and fat-stock beast together,
with a little boy to lead them.
The cow and the bear will graze,
their young will lie down together.
The lion will eat hay like the ox.
The infant will play over the hole of the adder,
the baby will put its hand into the viper's lair.
No hurt, no harm will be done on all my holy mountain,

for the land will be full of knowledge of the Lord,
as the waters cover the sea.
That day, the root of Jesse,
standing as a signal for the peoples,
will be sought out by the nations
and its dwelling will be glorious.

In the final verses of chapter 10, which immediately precede this passage, we hear of the Lord God's judgement on tall and proud trees, which symbolise powerful and arrogant rulers. The contrast with the 'branch which will spring from the stock of Jesse' is striking. God can use this humble descendant of David, filling him with the multiple gifts of the Spirit, so that he gives good judgment, especially for the poor and the weak, and 'strikes the violent with the rod of his mouth.' The establishment of 'righteousness' (*sedeq*) brings in its wake ecological harmony, as animals hitherto antagonistic become peaceable, and a little boy leads them. There will be 'no hurt, no harm' on God's holy mountain, for the land will be 'full of the knowledge of the Lord.' A second and similar image concludes the passage: the root of Jesse will be a 'signal for the peoples,' a banner to rally them. The Messiah arising from Israel and sent to Israel has nevertheless a universal role: his dwelling among the nations will reveal God's glory (*kabod*).

Psalm 72 (71) The Messiah will bring peace and justice. He will save the poor and the needy. 'All nations will bless his name.'

A reading from the letter of St Paul to the Romans (15:4-9)

Everything that was written earlier was written for our instruction so that we should have hope through perseverance and through the encouragement of the scriptures. May the God of perseverance and encouragement give you all the same purpose, following the example of Christ Jesus, so that, united in heart and mind, you may together give glory to the God and Father of our Lord Jesus Christ with one voice.

Accept one another, then, as Christ accepted you, for the glory of God. I tell you that Christ became a servant of the circumcised for the sake of God's truth, to confirm the promises made to our fathers, and so that the gentiles should give glory to God for his mercy, as it is written: *Therefore I shall praise you among the nations and sing praise to your name.*

PERSEVERANCE (*HUPOMONE*) AND encouragement (*paraklesis*) are gifts of God. Paul stresses that both gifts are derived from the holy Scriptures, given to God's people and handed on to Christians, gifts which bring hope. Paul prays that Christians may receive from the God of perseverance and encouragement the grace to follow 'the example of Christ Jesus'. This means accepting one another, 'for the glory of God'. Christ was first of all 'servant of the circumcised for the sake of God's truth', in order to be faithful to the promises made in earlier times regarding the nations (Genesis 12:3). Hence both Jew and Gentile come to praise God, as they acknowledge the mercy shown to them.

A reading from the holy gospel according to Matthew (3:1-12)

In those days, John the Baptist came, proclaiming in the desert of Judaea, saying, 'Repent, for the kingdom of Heaven has drawn near.' This was the man spoken of by the prophet Isaiah when he said:

> *A voice of one crying in the desert,*
> *Prepare a way for the Lord,*
> *make his paths straight.'*

John himself wore a garment of camel-hair with a leather belt round his waist, and his food was locusts and wild honey. Then Jerusalem and all Judaea and the whole region around the Jordan district kept going out to him, and they were baptised by him in the River Jordan as they confessed their sins. But seeing many of the Pharisees and Sadducees coming for baptism he said to them, 'Brood of vipers, who warned you to flee from the wrath to come? Produce fruit worthy of repentance, and do not be satisfied with saying to yourselves, "We have Abraham as our father," for I tell you, God can raise children for Abraham from these stones. Even now the axe is being laid to the root of the trees, so any tree failing to produce good fruit is cut down and thrown on the fire. I baptise you with water for repentance, but the one who comes after me is more powerful than I, and I am not fit to carry his sandals; he will baptise you with the Holy Spirit and fire. His winnowing-fan is in his hand; he will clear his threshing-floor and gather his wheat into his barn; but the chaff he will burn in a fire that never goes out.'

JOHN THE BAPTIST is always introduced to us on the Second Sunday of Advent. Matthew's account has John preach with the very same words Jesus will later use: 'Repent, for the kingdom of heaven has drawn near.' In this way Matthew stresses John's role as precursor. The evangelist uses words from the prophet Isaiah (40:3) to underline once again the fulfilment which comes with Jesus Christ. Specific to Matthew's account are John's fierce words to the Pharisees and Sadducees, when he calls them a 'brood of vipers', and speaks of 'the wrath to come'. Their being descendants of Abraham makes no difference. The image of the axe being prepared to fell trees which do not bear fruit, so that they can be consigned to the fire, continues the fierce tone which John assumes in Matthew's account. The coming Messiah will burn in fire the chaff separated from the wheat.

How do the fierce words of John the Baptist contrast with the tone of the preaching of Jesus?

Pray for the grace of repentance, and the willingness to begin again.

SECOND SUNDAY OF ADVENT – YEAR B

A reading from the prophet Isaiah (40:1-5, 9-11)

'Comfort, O comfort my people,'
says your God.
'Speak to the heart of Jerusalem
and cry out to her
that her period of service is ended,
her penalty has been paid;
from the hand of the Lord she has received
double for all her sins.'

A voice crying out,
'In the desert prepare a way for the Lord.
Make straight across the wastelands
a highway for our God.
Let every ravine be filled in,
every mountain and hill be brought down;
the crooked shall be straight,
the rough places a plain.
Then the glory of the Lord shall be revealed
and all humanity shall see it together,
for the mouth of the Lord has spoken.'

Go up on a high mountain, Zion,
herald of good news!
Lift up your voice with power, Jerusalem,
herald of good news!
Lift it up without fear!
Say to the cities of Judah,
'See, here is your God.'
See the Lord God coming with power,
his arm rules for him,
see, his reward is with him,
his prize goes before him.
He tends his flock like a shepherd,
gathering the lambs in his arms,
holding them against his breast
and leading the mother ewes.

THE SECOND PART of the book of Isaiah, chapters 40-55, opens with these consoling words addressed to the people, who have been exiled to Babylon. Their penalty has been paid. Something new is approaching. A first voice announces: 'prepare the way (*derek*)', so that God may come to lead the people back along a highway prepared for them. God does not just speak. God acts. God travels with people. Human beings will see 'the glory (*kabod*) of God'. Then the voice of Sion is summoned to deliver with power and without fear the good news, 'See, here is your God.' God comes with power, but also with tenderness, cradling the lambs at his breast. The 'second Isaiah' announces the gentle fidelity of God.

Psalm 85(84) The voice of God heralds peace. The glory of God 'dwells in our land'. Mercy and faithfulness connect this psalm with the 'good news' announced in the first reading.

A reading from the second letter of St Peter (3:8-14)

But one thing, beloved, you must never forget, is that with the Lord a day is like a thousand years, and a thousand years like a day. The Lord is not delaying his promises as some conceive delay, but he is being patient with you, not wanting anyone to be lost, but everyone to come to repentance. The Day of the Lord will come like a thief, and then with a roar the sky will vanish, the elements will catch fire and melt away, the earth and all that it contains will be revealed.

Since everything is coming to an end like this, what sort of people should you be, in holy conduct and devotion, while you wait for the day of God to come, eager for the coming of that day, on which the sky will dissolve in flames and the elements melt in the heat? In accordance with his promise let us wait for the new heavens and new earth, where righteousness is at home. So then, my dear friends, while you are waiting for these events, be eager to be found by him in peace, blameless and unsullied.

THESE CHRISTIANS ARE anxious that the return of Christ has been delayed. But God, who is beyond time, grants time for repentance and growth. When it does come, the Day (*hemera*) of the Lord will be sudden and dramatic. Christians should nevertheless be 'eager' for the Day, as they await 'the new heavens and new earth', living 'in peace, blameless and unsullied'.

A reading from the holy gospel according to Mark (1:1-8)

The beginning of the gospel about Jesus the Messiah, Son of God.

As it is written in the prophet Isaiah:

Look, I am sending my messenger in front of you
who will prepare your way.

A voice of one crying in the desert:
Prepare a way for the Lord,
make his paths straight.

John the Baptist was in the desert, proclaiming a baptism of repentance for the forgiveness of sins. All Judaea and all the people of Jerusalem were going out to him, and they were baptised by him in the River Jordan as they confessed their sins. John wore a garment of camel-skin, and a leather belt round his waist, and he ate locusts and wild honey. And as he proclaimed he said, 'After me is coming the one who is more powerful than me, and I am not fit to kneel down and undo the strap of his sandals. I have baptised you with water, but he will baptise you with the Holy Spirit.'

THESE ARE THE opening words of the Gospel according to Mark, the first words of the first gospel to be written. The evangelist proclaims Jesus as the Messiah, and Son of God, and straightaway adds the words of the prophet from our first reading. The time of fulfilment has come and the voice of John the Baptist is indeed the 'voice of one crying in the desert'. Mark goes on to describe the ministry of John the Baptist. 'Repentance' is not simply sorrow for sin, but commitment to a change of behaviour. John, who is dressed in the style of the prophet Elijah (2 Kings 1), accompanies his preaching with the ritual of baptism, performed in the river Jordan, but he explains that his baptism with water is simply a preparation for the one who is coming, whom John describes as 'more powerful than me', and who will baptise 'with the Holy Spirit'.

Why does John call Jesus 'more powerful'?
Pray for the readiness to change.

SECOND SUNDAY OF ADVENT – YEAR C

A reading from the prophet Baruch (5:1-9)

'Jerusalem, take off your garb of sorrow and distress,
put on for evermore the beauty of God's glory,

wrap around you the cloak of God's righteousness;
put on your head the diadem of the glory of the Eternal,
for God will show your splendour to every nation under heaven
and the name God gives you for evermore will be,
"Peace-through-Righteousness", and "Glory-through-Devotion".
Arise, Jerusalem, stand on the heights
and turn your eyes to the east:
see your children reassembled
from the setting of the sun to its rising
at the word of the Holy One,
rejoicing because God has remembered them.
Though they left you on foot, dragged off by enemies,
now God brings them back to you,
carried gloriously like a royal throne.
For God has decreed that each high mountain
should be brought low,
the everlasting hills and valleys
should be filled and the ground levelled
so that Israel can walk safely in the glory of God.
The glades and every fragrant tree
will provide shade for Israel at God's command;
for God will lead Israel with joy in the light of his glory,
with the mercy and righteousness which come from him.'

THE BOOK OF Baruch, written in post-exilic times, and preserved in the Greek Bible, takes up the themes of the second Isaiah. The whole passage is addressed to Jerusalem. She is called upon to dress herself with God's 'glory' (*doxa*) and God's 'righteousness' (*dikaiosune*). The time of mourning is over. She will be displayed by God to the nations, and receive new names. Her children are returning from exile, from east and west (Isaiah 49). They rejoice 'because God has remembered them'. As announced in Isaiah 40, the mountains will be levelled and the valleys filled. Trees will provide shade for the travelling people 'at God's command'. God's final gifts are 'the light of his glory', 'mercy' (*eleemosune*) and 'righteousness'. The themes of Advent are beautifully presented in this text.

Psalm 126(125) celebrates the return from exile, and the marvels worked by God. Tears are replaced by laughter and song.

A reading from the letter of St Paul to the Philippians (1:3-6, 8-11)

I thank my God every time I remember you, and in every prayer of mine for you all. I pray with joy at your partnership in the gospel from the first day until now, confident that the One who began good work in you will bring it to completion by the Day of Christ Jesus. For God is my witness how much I long for you all with the affection of Christ Jesus; and this I pray, that your love for one another may overflow more and more with knowledge and complete understanding that will enable you to discern what is best, so that you may be innocent and blameless for the Day of Christ, filled with the fruit of righteousness through Jesus Christ, for the glory and praise of God.

PAUL HAD A particular affection for the Christians of Philippi. He tells them that when he prays for them he prays always 'with joy'. They have been constant in their faith right from the start, and God will bring to perfection the good work begun in them for the 'day' (*hemera*) of Christ Jesus. Paul's commitment to them reflects the depth of feeling of Christ Jesus, and he prays that their love (*agape*) will grow stronger with greater knowledge and understanding. On the 'day' of Christ they will be 'innocent and blameless', filled with the 'fruit of righteousness (*dikaiosune*)', that gift of God, which they receive 'through Jesus Christ', 'to the glory and praise of God'.

A reading from the holy gospel according to Luke (3:1-6)

In the fifteenth year of the rule of Tiberius Caesar, when Pontius Pilate was governor of Judaea, Herod tetrarch of Galilee, his brother Philip tetrarch of the territories of Ituraea and Trachonitis, Lysanias tetrarch of Abilene, during the high-priesthood of Annas and Caiaphas, the word of God came to John, the son of Zechariah, in the desert. He went into the whole Jordan area proclaiming a baptism of repentance for the forgiveness of sins, as it is written in the book of the sayings of Isaiah the prophet:

A voice of one crying in the desert:
Prepare a way for the Lord,
make his paths straight!
Every valley shall be filled in,
every mountain and hill be levelled,
the crooked shall be straightened
and rough places made into smooth roads,
and all flesh shall see the salvation of God.

LUKE'S INTRODUCTION OF John the Baptist goes to great lengths to place him in the context of contemporary rulers, both secular and religious. Luke also has the 'word of God' coming to John as to a prophet. In the words of Jesus, John is a prophet, and 'more than a prophet' (Luke 7:26). He proclaims 'a baptism of repentance for the forgiveness of sins'. John also fulfils the prophecy of Isaiah 40, and Luke extends the quotation, already used from that chapter by Mark and Matthew, to include the levelling of hills and mountains and the filling in of the valleys, all in preparation for the coming of the Lord. This allows him to reach Isaiah's words 'and all flesh shall see the salvation of God'. Luke is concerned to point out that the Messiah will come for the salvation of all nations.

What is special in Luke's presentation of John the Baptist?
God works amid the complex events of human history.

MONDAY OF THE SECOND WEEK IN ADVENT

A reading from the prophet Isaiah (35:1-10)

Let the desert and the arid lands be glad,
let the wasteland rejoice and bloom;
let it burst into flower like the crocus,
let it rejoice and sing for joy.
The glory of Lebanon shall be given to it,
the splendour of Carmel and Sharon;
they shall see the glory of the Lord,

the splendour of our God.
Strengthen all weary hands,
steady all trembling knees
and say to the faint-hearted,
'Be strong! Do not be afraid.
Here is your God,
vengeance is coming, divine retribution;
he is coming to save you.'
Then the eyes of the blind will be opened,
the ears of the deaf unsealed,
then the lame will leap like a deer
and the tongue of the dumb sing for joy;
for water will burst forth in the desert
and streams in arid lands,
parched ground will become a marsh
and thirsty land springs of water;
lairs where the jackals used to live
will become plots of reed and rushes.
And through it will run a highway
which will be called the Sacred Way.
The unclean will not be allowed to use it:
it shall be for God's people
and the fool will not stray along it.
No lion will be there,
no predator set foot on it,
none shall be found there;
the redeemed shall walk there.
Those ransomed by the Lord shall return
and come to Zion shouting for joy,
crowned with joy unending;
rejoicing and gladness will escort them
and sorrow and sighing will take flight.

THE HEALING OF the natural world and the healing of human beings are intertwined in this poem. As so often in the second part of Isaiah, for example in chapter 41, so also here the desert becomes fertile. The tone is especially exuberant, for the 'glory' (*kabod*) of the Lord, the 'splendour' (*hadar*) of our

God, glimpsed in Lebanon, Carmel and Sharon, is now revealed. The faint-hearted are consoled, the blind see, the deaf hear, the lame walk, and the dumb speak. Once the land becomes fertile, a 'Sacred Way' (*derek haqqodesh*) is made for God's people, where there is complete safety to return to Sion, 'shouting for joy'. The passage anticipates the poems of the second Isaiah. As in Isaiah 49, Sion's children will return from the nations. 'Sorrow and sighing' are at an end.

Psalm 85 (84) God comes to save. 'Justice marches before him', and 'peace follows his steps'.

A reading from the holy gospel according to Luke (5:17-26)

Now it happened that he was teaching one day, and Pharisees and teachers of the Law, who had come from every village in Galilee, from Judaea and from Jerusalem, were sitting there. And the power of the Lord was there that he should heal. And now some men came, bringing on a bed a paralysed man whom they were trying to bring in and lay down in front of him. But as they could find no way of getting the man through the crowd, they went up onto the top of the house and lowered him and his stretcher down through the tiles into the middle, in front of Jesus. Seeing their faith he said, 'My friend, your sins are forgiven you.' The scribes and the Pharisees began to discuss this: 'Who is this man, talking blasphemy? Who but God alone can forgive sins?' But Jesus, aware of their thoughts, made them this reply, 'What are you discussing in your hearts? Which of these is easier: to say, "Your sins are forgiven you," or to say, "Get up and walk"? But so that you may know that the Son of man has authority on earth to forgive sins,' – he said to the paralysed man – 'I order you: get up, and pick up your stretcher and go home.' And immediately before their eyes he got up, picked up what he had been lying on and went home glorifying God. They were all astounded and glorified God and were filled with awe, saying, 'We have seen strange things today.'

WHILE THE ISAIAH reading described the healing of the earth and of human lives, the gospel focuses on one man. The paralysed man takes no part in the healing. It is the faith of his friends which Jesus 'sees', lavishly giving healing to the sick man. He is the recipient of the power of God through Jesus, firstly as his sins are forgiven and his heart healed. His getting up and going home confirms that Jesus does indeed have power to heal the whole person. The religious leaders seem unwilling to acknowledge that God's healing can be bestowed in this way, but the people are ecstatic. They are more open to the surprises God can work.

How might religious faith close our minds to the surprises of God? God works for our good even when we are unaware of God's power.

TUESDAY OF THE SECOND WEEK IN ADVENT

A reading from the prophet Isaiah (40:1-11)

'Comfort, O comfort my people,'
says your God.
'Speak to the heart of Jerusalem
and cry out to her
that her period of service is ended,
her penalty has been paid;
from the hand of the Lord she has received
double for all her sins.'
A voice crying out,
'In the desert prepare a way for the Lord.
Make straight across the wastelands
a highway for our God.
Let every ravine be filled in,
every mountain and hill be brought down;
the crooked shall be straight,
the rough places a plain.
Then the glory of the Lord shall be revealed
and all humanity shall see it together,
for the mouth of the Lord has spoken.'
A voice said, 'Cry aloud!'
and I said, 'What shall I cry?'

'All humanity is grass
and all its beauty like the wild flower.
The grass withers, the flower fades
when the breath of the Lord blows on them.
(The grass is surely the people.)
Grass withers, a flower fades,
but the word of our God stands firm for ever.'
Go up on a high mountain, Zion,
herald of good news!
Lift up your voice with power, Jerusalem,
herald of good news!
Lift it up without fear!
Say to the cities of Judah,
'See, here is your God.'
See the Lord God coming with power,
his arm rules for him,
see, his reward is with him,
his prize goes before him.
He tends his flock like a shepherd,
gathering the lambs in his arms,
holding them against his breast
and leading the mother ewes.

NO FEWER THAN three voices mark this opening text of the second Isaiah. The voice 'crying out' commands that a way be prepared for God. Ravines are to be filled in and hills brought low. The text is familiar because it is used in the gospels in relation to the ministry of John the Baptist. A second voice cries out that 'humanity is grass', and that only the 'word of our God' stands for ever. God's word gives life and allows human beings to thrive. This prepares us for the third voice, that of Jerusalem, which delivers the message, the good news, that God is 'coming with power'. God will accompany his people as they return home from exile on the way prepared for them, showing tenderness and compassion like a loving shepherd. The three voices are one in proclaiming the coming of God to save.

Psalm 96 (95) The psalm too announces the coming of the Lord, as he 'comes to rule the earth'. The whole of creation welcomes God in rejoicing, and the message is for 'all the peoples'.

A reading from the holy gospel according to Matthew (18:12-14)

Jesus said to his disciples: 'What do you think? If a man has a hundred sheep and one of them strays; will he not leave the ninety-nine in the mountains and go in search of the stray? Amen I say to you, if he finds it, he rejoices more over it than over the ninety-nine that did not stray. Similarly, it is never the will of your Father in heaven that one of these little ones should be lost.

THE GOSPEL TAKES up the image of God as shepherd which occurred at the end of the Isaiah reading. The short parable of the lost sheep occurs in Luke 15 with two other parables, the lost coin and the lost son, all of them about God's rejoicing on the return of the sinner. Here in Matthew's gospel this parable is part of Jesus' discourse about community. It teaches that the community is the place where forgiveness and care for the lost should be practised.

Should we seek out the lost, or wait for them to return?
God's good news of salvation is especially relevant for those who are lost.

WEDNESDAY OF THE SECOND WEEK IN ADVENT

A reading from the prophet Isaiah (40:25-31)

'To whom can you compare me, or who is my equal?'
says the Holy One.
Lift up your eyes and see who created them.
He leads out their army in order,

summoning each one of them by name.
So mighty is his power, so great his strength,
not one of them fails to appear.
Why can you say, Jacob,
why do you proclaim, Israel,
'My way is hidden from the Lord,
my cause is ignored by my God'?
Do you not know? Have you not heard?
The Lord is the God of ages,
he created the furthest ends of the earth.
He does not grow tired or weary,
his understanding cannot be fathomed.
He gives force to the weary,
he strengthens the powerless.
Youths may grow tired and weary,
young people stumble and fall,
but those who hope in the Lord will renew their strength,
they will grow wings like eagles,
they will run and not grow weary,
walk but never tire.

GOD CHALLENGES THE people: 'to whom can you compare me?' God is the one who creates the heavens; the stars appear at his bidding. God then challenges these exiles for their despondency, as they repeatedly claim that God is ignoring their plight. The response affirms that God is not only creator but also sustainer of the people. God is tireless, with more energy than the young, who still grow weary and fall. This means that those who trust in God's power and will to save 'will grow wings like eagles'. They will 'never tire'.

Psalm 103 (102) The psalm too describes the qualities of God, who is forgiving, compassionate and loving, 'slow to anger and rich in mercy' (Exodus 34).

A reading from the holy gospel according to Matthew (11:28-30)

Jesus exclaimed: 'Come to me, all you who labour and are overburdened, and I will give you rest. Take my yoke upon you and learn from me, for I am gentle and humble in heart, and *you will find rest for your souls.* For my yoke is easy and my burden light.'

THIS IS THE second part of a speech of Jesus. The first part is a prayer addressed to the Father 'Lord of heaven and earth', in which Jesus thanks God for revealing the good news to the 'infants'. In the second part, the verses of this gospel reading, Jesus speaks to those who 'labour and are overburdened'. Jesus will, like the shepherd, lead them to rest. The God who never tires of leading his people to freedom is revealed in Jesus who is 'gentle and humble in heart', and who offers a yoke that is light.

What does it mean to be 'humble in heart'?
The 'rest' of God is offered to all.

THURSDAY OF THE SECOND WEEK IN ADVENT

A reading from the prophet Isaiah (41:13-20)

For I, the Lord your God,
I grasp you by your right hand;
I tell you, 'Do not be afraid, I shall be your help.'
Do not be afraid, you worm Jacob,
you insect Israel!
'I shall be your help,'
– declares the Lord;
your redeemer is the Holy One of Israel.
Look, I am making of you a threshing-sledge,
sharp, new, equipped with teeth.
You will thresh the mountains to dust
and reduce the hills to chaff.
You will winnow them and the wind will carry them off,

the gale will scatter them;
but you will rejoice in the Lord,
will glory in the Holy One of Israel.
The oppressed and needy search for water,
and there is none,
their tongue is parched with thirst.
I the Lord will provide for them.
I the God of Israel will not abandon them.
I shall open up rivers on bare heights
and waterholes among the ravines;
I shall turn the desert into a lake
and dry ground into springs of water.
I shall place cedar trees in the desert,
acacias, myrtles and olives;
in the wastelands I shall put cypress trees,
plane trees and pine together,
so that people may see and know,
so that they may all observe and understand
that the hand of the Lord has done this,
that the Holy One of Israel has created it.

THE PROPHET IS called to announce to the exiles that God, who 'grasps you by your right hand' is ready to bring them back home. 'Do not be afraid', says the Lord, to the 'worm' Jacob, to the 'insect' Israel. These strange ways of addressing the people simply underline their helplessness when left to their own devices. God will transform them into a 'threshing-sledge', another unique image, but now one of strength. They will resume control of their own destiny. The second half of this passage takes up again the common themes of second Isaiah, providing for the needy, and transforming creation for the benefit of people. An extraordinary list of shrubs illustrates the generosity of God. All this is what the 'hand of the Lord' can do.

Psalm 145 (144) God is 'king', and his name is blessed. His reign lasts 'from age to age'.

A reading from the holy gospel according to Matthew (11:11-15)

Jesus spoke to the crowds: 'Amen I say to you, of the children born to women, none has been raised up greater than John the Baptist; yet the least in the kingdom of Heaven is greater than he. Since John the Baptist came, up to this present time, the kingdom of Heaven has been subjected to violence and the violent are taking it by storm. For all the prophets and the Law prophesied until John the Baptist; and he, if you will accept it, is Elijah who was to come. Anyone who has ears should listen!'

THE GOSPEL READINGS on Advent weekdays constantly refer to John the Baptist from this point. Jesus' words about the greatness of John are qualified by reference to those in the kingdom of heaven, who, Jesus continues, are all even greater. John is the last of the long line of prophets, indeed he is 'Elijah who was to come', as suggested in the book of Malachi chapter 3. The figure of Elijah and his fierce commitment to the true God are a fitting model for John. The 'violence' needed by those who enter the kingdom may be interpreted as their single-minded commitment, for those who enter it are even more determined than John.

How committed am I to entering the kingdom of Heaven?
Striving for the kingdom should be our first priority.

FRIDAY OF THE SECOND WEEK IN ADVENT

A reading from the prophet Isaiah (48:17-19)

Thus says the Lord, your redeemer,
the Holy One of Israel,
'I am the Lord your God
and teach you for your own good;
I lead you in the way you should go.
If only you had listened to my commandments!
Your prosperity would have been like a river

and your righteousness like the waves of the sea.
Your descendants would have been numbered like the sand,
your offspring as many as its grains.
Their name would never be cut off
or blotted out from my presence.'

THE LORD IS presented as 'redeemer' (*go'el*), the one who buys back his people's freedom, and, as so often throughout Isaiah, as 'holy one' (*qadosh*). The Lord presents himself as 'your God', as 'one who teaches' and as 'one who leads', who instructs people on the good way to be followed. The climax of the passage is God's words of regret: 'if only you had listened to my commandments (*mitswot)*'. A whole set of images then follows: your prosperity (*shalom*) would have been 'like a river', your righteousness (*tsedaqah*) 'like the waves of the sea', and, in a clear allusion to God's words to Abraham (Genesis 22), your descendants would have been 'like the sand', and your offspring 'like grain'. Instead of the misery of destruction and exile they have suffered, their name would never be 'cut off' or 'blotted out'. This is the lesson they must learn.

Psalm 1 The psalm presents the choice announced in the reading: to delight in the law of the Lord, or to follow the 'counsel of the wicked'.

A reading from the holy gospel according to Matthew (11:16-19)

Jesus spoke to the crowds: 'With whom can I compare this generation? It is like children shouting to the others as they sit in the market place, "We played the pipes for you, and you wouldn't dance; we sang dirges, and you wouldn't beat your breasts." For John came, neither eating nor drinking, and they say, "He is possessed." The Son of man came, eating and drinking, and they say, "Look, a glutton and a drunkard, a friend of tax collectors and sinners." Yet wisdom is justified by her deeds.'

THESE VERSES FOLLOW immediately from yesterday's gospel, and John the Baptist is once again mentioned. Jesus presents a parable about petulant children in the market place by which he describes 'this generation', the crowds who follow him. Whatever they do, whatever behaviour they pursue, from playing pipes to singing dirges, they always complain. Similarly both the ascetic style of John and the convivial behaviour of Jesus are rejected, both giving rise to criticism. This generation cannot be satisfied, for they are unwilling to 'listen', yet 'wisdom is justified by her deeds', and the work of God through John and Jesus will achieve its end.

Am I like the children in the parable, never satisfied?
We need a readiness to respond, however strange God's ways may seem.

SATURDAY OF THE SECOND WEEK IN ADVENT

A reading from the book of Ecclesiasticus (48:1-4,9-11)

Then the prophet Elijah arose like a fire,
his word flaring like a torch.
It was he who brought famine on them,
in his zeal he made them few in number.
By the word of the Lord he shut up the heavens;
three times also he brought down fire.
How glorious you were in your miracles, Elijah!
Has anyone reason to boast like you? –
taken up in the whirlwind of fire,
in a chariot with fiery horses,
designated in the prophecies in due time
to allay God's wrath before the fury,
to turn the hearts of fathers towards their children
and to restore the tribes of Jacob.
Blessed those who will see you
and those who have fallen asleep in love –
for we too shall have life.

THE BOOK OF Ecclesiasticus, the Wisdom of Ben Sira, preserved in the Greek Bible, though originally written in Hebrew, concludes with several chapters of 'praise of the ancestors'. Among them is the prophet Elijah. It is of special interest that he was 'taken up in the whirlwind of fire'. The prophet Malachi speaks of the return of Elijah to be a preacher of reconciliation (3:23-24), a text which is clearly in the mind of Ben Sira. The final verse of our passage speaks of the blessed state of those who see Elijah, and those who have 'fallen asleep in love'. There is a hint here of personal immortality.

Psalm 80 (79) The Hebrew refrain of this psalm has God, the 'shepherd of Israel', being asked to bring the people back, and to allow his 'face' to shine, so that they may be saved. The refrain of the Hebrew psalm becomes our response.

A reading from the holy gospel according to Matthew (17:10-13)

The disciples put this question to Jesus, 'Why then do the scribes say that Elijah must come first?' He replied, 'Elijah is indeed coming, and he will set everything right again; however, I tell you that Elijah has come already and they did not recognise him, but they did what they liked with him; and the Son of man will suffer similarly at their hands.' Then the disciples understood that he was speaking of John the Baptist.

THESE VERSES OF conversation follow Matthew's account of the transfiguration, in which Moses and Elijah have appeared with Jesus. Jesus confirms what the scribes teach, that Elijah will return 'to set everything right', and furthermore asserts that Elijah has already returned in the person of John the Baptist. Both Elijah and John spoke up for the truth, and suffered for it. Jesus goes on to say that he himself, 'the Son of man', will suffer in a similar way.

How does the ministry of John reflect that of Elijah?
Both John and Jesus suffer martyrdom for the truth.

THIRD SUNDAY OF ADVENT – YEAR A

A reading from the prophet Isaiah (35:1-6,10)

Let the desert and the arid lands be glad,
let the wasteland rejoice and bloom;
let it burst into flower like the crocus,
let it rejoice and sing for joy.
The glory of Lebanon shall be given to it,
the splendour of Carmel and Sharon;
they shall see the glory of the Lord,
the splendour of our God.
Strengthen all weary hands,
steady all trembling knees
and say to the faint-hearted,
'Be strong! Do not be afraid.
Here is your God,
vengeance is coming, divine retribution;
he is coming to save you.'
Then the eyes of the blind will be opened,
the ears of the deaf unsealed,
then the lame will leap like a deer
and the tongue of the dumb sing for joy;
for water will burst forth in the desert
and streams in arid lands,
Those ransomed by the Lord shall return
and come to Zion shouting for joy,
crowned with joy unending;
rejoicing and gladness will escort them
and sorrow and sighing will take flight.

ON THIS THIRD Sunday of Advent the joyful tone is taken up by these verses from the prophet Isaiah. The final verse even speaks of 'joy unending' (*simhat 'olam*). A journey back to Sion is described, in which 'God is coming to save you.' The 'glory' (*kabod)* of God and God's 'splendour' (*hadar*) are to be seen, a reason for courage and strength. Various human disabilities are healed: the blind see, the deaf hear, the lame leap, the dumb sing. The created environment is renewed as water bursts out in the desert. The 'ransomed' will return to the holy city, amid bursts of rejoicing, while 'sorrow and sighing will take flight'.

> **Psalm 146 (145)** The Lord 'keeps faith', and can be relied upon to save the oppressed, the stranger, the widow and the orphan.

A reading from the letter of St James (5:7-10)

Now be patient, brothers and sisters, until the Lord's coming. See how a farmer waits patiently for the precious fruit of the earth until it receives the autumn rain and the spring rain. You too must be patient; do not lose heart, because the Lord's coming is near. Do not make complaints against one another, brothers and sisters, so as not to be brought to judgement yourselves; see, the judge is standing at the gates. For your example of patience in persecution take the prophets who spoke in the Lord's name.

THE ADVENT THEME of the Lord's coming (*parousia*) is found again in the letter of James, a New Testament book which is akin to the wisdom writings of the Hebrew scriptures. He echoes the teaching of Jesus about the Lord's coming (Mark 13), and stresses above all the need to 'be patient' (*makrothumein*), by imitating the farmer who awaits good fruit from his land. James also offers the example of 'patience in persecution' of the prophets.

A reading from the holy gospel according to Matthew (11:2-11)

Now John had heard in prison what the Messiah was doing and he sent his disciples to ask him, 'Are you the one who is to come, or are we to expect someone else?' Jesus answered, 'Go back and tell John what you hear and see; the blind see again, and the lame walk, lepers are cleansed, and the deaf hear, the dead are raised to life and the good news is proclaimed to the poor; and blessed is anyone who does not find me a cause of stumbling.' As the men were leaving, Jesus began to talk to the people about John, 'What did you go out into the desert to see? A reed swaying in the breeze? Then what did you go out to see?

Someone wearing fine clothes? Look, those who wear fine clothes are to be found in royal palaces. Then what did you go out for? To see a prophet? Yes, I tell you, and more than a prophet. This is the one of whom it is written:

> *Look, I am going to send my messenger ahead of you to prepare the way before you.*

'Amen I say to you, of the children born to women, none has been raised up greater than John the Baptist; yet the least in the kingdom of Heaven is greater than he.'

A FURTHER GOSPEL about John the Baptist is taken from the time of his imprisonment by Herod the tetrarch. The response given by Jesus to the question John is asking points to his healings. It ends with the interesting words: 'blessed is the one who does not find in me a cause of stumbling (*skandalizein*)'. It seems that John is troubled for he may have expected a more challenging style from Jesus. In Matthew 3:12 John talks about the Messiah 'burning chaff'. But Jesus shows a merciful outreach to those in need, and 'the good news is proclaimed to the poor'. If this may seem like a veiled rebuke from Jesus, it is followed immediately by words about John's greatness: he is 'greater than a prophet' and no child born of women is greater than he, though 'the least in the kingdom' is greater still.

Can you see beyond the apparent contradiction in Jesus' final words? John the Baptist, like all of us, has to learn the lesson of mercy.

THIRD SUNDAY OF ADVENT – YEAR B

A reading from the prophet Isaiah (61:1-2, 10-11)

The spirit of Lord God is on me
for the Lord has anointed me.
He has sent me to bring good news to the afflicted,
to soothe the broken-hearted,

to proclaim liberty to captives,
release to those in prison,
to proclaim a year of the Lord's favour.
I exult for joy in the Lord,
my soul rejoices in my God
for he has clothed me in garments of salvation,
he has wrapped me in a cloak of saving justice,
like a bridegroom wearing his garland,
like a bride adorned in her jewels.
For as the earth sends up its shoots
and a garden makes seeds flourish,
so the Lord God makes saving justice and praise
flourish in the sight of all nations.

THIS PROPHET IS deeply aware of the gift of the spirit of the Lord, and that he has been anointed to bring 'good news', and to proclaim a year of jubilee, a year 'of the Lord's favour'. The message of comfort was first proclaimed in Isaiah 40 as the exiles were told of their release from Babylon and restoration to their land. It is not surprising that the words of this reading are found on the lips of Jesus when he visits the Nazareth synagogue (Luke 4). The second half of the reading personifies the whole people, who 'exult for joy in the Lord', who has clothed them in 'salvation' (*yesha'*) and 'saving justice' (*tsedaqah*). The work of the Lord in liberating his people is witnessed by 'all nations', and is compared to the earth 'sending up shoots' and a garden 'making seeds flourish'.

Luke 1 The 'responsorial psalm' uses verses from the Magnificat, as Mary rejoices and proclaims the greatness of the Lord. It reflects the exultation of the people.

A reading from the first letter of St Paul to the Thessalonians (5:16-24)

Always be joyful; pray constantly; in every situation give thanks; this is the will of God for you in Christ Jesus. Do not stifle the Spirit or treat prophecy with contempt; test everything and hold fast to what is good, and *shun every* form of *evil.*

May the God of peace sanctify you fully; and may your spirit, life and body be kept blameless for the coming of our Lord Jesus Christ. He who has called you is trustworthy and will carry it out.

THESE WORDS COME towards the end of this earliest of Paul's letters. The theme of joy (*chairein*) is maintained, for to be joyful is part of 'the will of God in Christ Jesus'. A series of imperatives is put forward. Paul ends with a prayer to the 'God of peace' that the whole person, 'spirit (*pneuma*), life (*psyche*) and body (*soma*)', be ready for the coming (*parousia*) of the Lord. The God who calls is 'trustworthy' (*pistos*), and will fulfil the promise.

A reading from the holy gospel according to John (1:6-8, 19-28)

There was a man sent by God.
His name was John.
He came as a witness,
to bear witness to the light,
so that everyone might believe through him.
He was not the light,
he was to bear witness to the light.

This is the witness of John, when the Jews sent to him priests and Levites from Jerusalem to ask him, 'Who are you?' He declared, he did not deny but declared, 'I am not the Messiah.' So they asked, 'What then? Are you Elijah?' He replied, 'I am not.' 'Are you the Prophet?' He answered, 'No.' So they said to him, 'Who are you? So that we may give an answer to those who sent us. What do you say about yourself?' So he said, 'I am, as Isaiah prophesied:

A voice of one that cries in the desert:
prepare a way for the Lord.'

Now they had been sent from the Pharisees, and they put a question to him and said, 'Why then are you baptising if you are not the Messiah nor Elijah nor the Prophet?' John answered them, 'I baptise with water; but among you is standing one whom you do not know, the one who is coming after me; and I am not worthy to undo the strap of his sandal.'

This happened at Bethany, on the far side of the Jordan, where John was baptising.

TWO SEPARATE SECTIONS of the first chapter of John's gospel are joined together here by the word 'witness' (*marturia*). The 'man sent by God' is John the Baptist, who was not the 'light' (*phos*), but a 'witness' for the light. The text then omits ten verses and tells how John bears 'witness' to the priests and Levites who came down from Jerusalem. John declares that he is not the Messiah, not Elijah and not the expected prophet. In words originating from Isaiah 40 and familiar from their use in the other gospels, he declares that he is 'a voice' (*phone*) which cries out. He offers a baptism of water, in readiness for 'the one who is coming'. In putting together these verses from chapter one of John the lectionary provides a clear idea of the mission of the Baptist.

How far would you consider your own life to be bearing witness?
The one who bears witness may become the martyr who gives life away.

THIRD SUNDAY OF ADVENT – YEAR C

A reading from the prophet Zephaniah (3:14-18)

Shout for joy, daughter Zion,
Israel, shout aloud!
Rejoice, exult with all your heart, daughter Jerusalem!
The Lord has removed your sentence;
he has turned your enemy away.
The Lord is king among you, Israel:
you have nothing more to fear.
On that Day, it will be said to Jerusalem,
'Zion, have no fear, do not let your hands fall limp.'
The Lord your God is within you,
the saving warrior.
He will rejoice over you with gladness,
he will renew you in his love,

he will dance with shouts of joy for you
as on a day of festival.
I have taken away your misfortune,
I no longer need you to bear the disgrace of it.

THESE WORDS COME towards the end of the book of the prophet Zephaniah, and round the book off with psalms of joy. In words reminiscent of Isaiah 40, which proclaimed that the 'penalty has been paid', Zephaniah declares that the sentence (*mishpat*) has been 'removed'. The Lord is 'king' among the people, who are told there is nothing more to fear. The Lord himself is a saving 'warrior' who will rejoice, renewing Israel with his love, and dancing with joy, because Sion's 'misfortune' has ended.

Isaiah 12 This short chapter of Isaiah serves as a responsorial psalm. It proclaims God as 'my salvation' and speaks of drawing water 'joyfully from the springs of salvation'.

A reading from the letter of St Paul to the Philippians (4:4-7)

Rejoice in the Lord always; I say again, rejoice. Let your good sense be known to everyone. The Lord is near. Do not worry about anything; but in every prayer and petition make your requests known to God with thanksgiving, and the peace of God which is beyond all understanding will guard your hearts and your thoughts in Christ Jesus.

REMEMBERING THE AFFECTION of the Christians of Philippi, Paul urges them to rejoice (*chairein*) constantly. The opening words of this reading have become prominent in the liturgy of this day, which is consequently known as *Gaudete* Sunday. The Philippians are filled with joy because they have received 'good sense' from the Lord, and the Lord is near. There is an insistence on prayer and thanksgiving. Their confidence in the goodness of God means that the 'peace (*eirene*) of God', which surpasses understanding, will guard them 'in Christ Jesus'.

A reading from the holy gospel according to Luke (3:10-18)

And the crowds asked John, 'What should we do, then?' He answered them, saying, 'Anyone who has two tunics must share with the one who has none, and anyone who has food must do the same.' Tax collectors, too, came to be baptised, and they said to him, 'Teacher, what should we do?' He said to them, 'Collect no more than the rate appointed for you.' Soldiers also asked him, 'What about us? What should we do?' He said to them, 'No intimidation! No false accusation! Be content with your pay!'

There was a feeling of expectancy among the people; they were all questioning in their hearts whether John might himself be the Messiah. John answered them all by saying, 'I baptise you with water, but one more powerful than me is coming, and I am not fit to undo the strap of his sandals; he will baptise you with the Holy Spirit and with fire. His winnowing-fan is in his hand, to clear his threshing-floor and to gather the wheat into his barn; but the chaff he will burn in a fire that never goes out.' And he proclaimed the good news to the people with many other exhortations too.

JOHN'S PREACHING ABOUT the 'wrath to come' (3:7) is followed by words from different groups with the repeated question, 'what should we do?' Only Luke gives these details. His first instruction, in keeping with prophetic custom, is that clothes and food should be shared with the needy. Tax collectors are told to collect the proper rate of tax, not lining their pockets. Soldiers are told not to intimidate, or accuse falsely and to be content with their pay. The expectancy among the crowd raises the question of John's real mission, leading him to speak of the baptism of the one who is 'more powerful' which will be given 'with the Holy Spirit and with fire'. John also expects that the Messiah will 'burn the chaff in a fire that never goes out'. Luke says that, like Jesus, he 'proclaimed the good news' (*euaggelizesthai*) to the people.

Is John right to speak of the fire of judgement?
Each group, each person, needs to enquire: 'What should I do?'

MONDAY OF THE THIRD WEEK IN ADVENT

A reading from the book of Numbers (24:2-7, 15-17)

Raising his eyes Balaam saw Israel settled tribe by tribe; the spirit of God came on him and he declaimed his poem, saying:

'The oracle of Balaam son of Beor,
the oracle of the man whose eye is clear,
the oracle of one who hears the words of God.
He sees what Shaddai makes him see,
He may fall, but his eyes are open.
How fair are your tents, O Jacob,
your dwellings, O Israel,
like valleys that stretch afar,
like gardens by the banks of a river,
like aloes planted by the Lord,
like cedars beside the waters!
Water drips from his branches,
his seed is by many waters.
His king is greater than Agag,
and his kingship is held in honour.'
He then declaimed his poem, saying:
'The oracle of Balaam son of Beor,
the oracle of the man whose eye is clear,
the oracle of one who hears the words of God,
of one who knows the knowledge of the Most High.
He sees what Shaddai makes him see,
He may fall, but his eyes are open.
I see him – but not in the present.
I perceive him – but not close at hand:
a star issues from Jacob,
a sceptre arises from Israel.'

BALAAM IS A seer, sent by the king of Moab to curse Israel, which, during its wilderness journeying, is threatening to engulf his lands. Despite being a pagan, Balaam knows the Lord, whom he names with the ancient title

'Shaddai', and he receives 'the spirit of God'. It is not unusual that pagan eyes see the truth with new clarity. Using botanical imagery, he speaks of the beauty of Israel's tents encamped in the desert. Israel's 'king' (*melek*) is 'greater than Agag', the famed king of Amalek. In a second speech, introduced with the same solemnity, Balaam speaks of a 'star' (*kokab*) born of Israel and a 'sceptre' (*shebet)* arising from Jacob, but 'not in the present' and 'not close at hand'. Both speeches are quickly understood as containing references to a Messiah king, and this gave rise to Christian use of this text. Reference to a 'hero' in earlier translations of the *Jerusalem Bible* derives from the Septuagint, the ancient Greek Bible, which struggled to understand the Hebrew of v.7 ('Water drips') and produced a different rendering.

Psalm 25 (24) In the psalm we ask God to 'remember' (zakar) his mercy and love, and to 'remember' us 'because of his goodness'.

A reading from the holy gospel according to Matthew (21:23-27)

Jesus had gone into the Temple and was teaching, when the chief priests and the elders of the people came to him and said, 'By what authority do you do these things? And who gave you this authority?' In reply Jesus said to them, 'I too will ask you a question; if you tell me the answer, then I will tell you by what authority I do these things. John's baptism: what was its origin, heavenly or human?' And they discussed among themselves, 'If we say "heavenly", he will reply to us, "Then why did you refuse to believe him?"; but if we say "human", we have the people to fear, for they all hold that John was a prophet.' So in answer to Jesus they said, 'We do not know.' And he replied to them, 'Neither will I tell you by what authority I do these things.'

THE PASSAGE FOLLOWS closely on the account of the 'cleansing' of the Temple, and that of the cursing of the barren fig tree, events which according to Matthew happened in the final days of the Jerusalem ministry of Jesus. The priests and elders ask about the authority (*exousia*) Jesus has to do 'these things'. This is a clever question, which tries to trick Jesus into claiming exalted status. They are determined to find something by which they can condemn him. Jesus sees their purpose, and asks a question in return, a question about the origin of the baptism of John the Baptist. The priests and elders are now faced with a trap. They cannot claim John's authority came from God, since they rejected him; and if they say it had human origin, they risk antagonizing the people. Their own authority is in shreds.

What is the purpose of the question of the chief priests and elders? To open one's mind to the new things of God is indeed a grace.

TUESDAY OF THE THIRD WEEK IN ADVENT

A reading from the book of Zephaniah *(3:1-2, 9-13)*

Woe to the rebellious, the befouled, the tyrannical city!
It did not listen to the call, did not accept correction;
it did not trust in the Lord, did not draw near to its God.
Yes, then I shall purge the lips of the peoples
so that all may invoke the name of the Lord
and serve him with one accord.
From beyond the rivers of Ethiopia,
my suppliants will bring me tribute.
When that Day comes you will never again
be ashamed of all the deeds
by which you once rebelled against me,
for I shall rid you of those who exult in your splendour;
never again will you preen yourself on my holy mountain.
But in you I shall leave surviving a humble and lowly people
and the remnant in Israel will take refuge
in the name of the Lord.
They will do no wrong, will tell no lies;
nor will a deceitful tongue be found in their mouths.
But they will graze and rest with no one to alarm them.

TWO SETS OF verses come from the third and final chapter of the minor prophet, Zephaniah, a contemporary of Jeremiah. The first section is a 'woe' speech against Jerusalem, dating before its destruction by the Babylonians. The people 'did not listen', trusting in political alliances and refusing to trust in the Lord, or draw near to God. These are common prophetic accusations. But the tone changes and God announces a new start, whereby God purges their lips so that they may invoke and serve the Lord. People will come 'from beyond the rivers of Ethiopia', from very distant lands. There remains 'a humble (*'ani*) and lowly (*dal*) people', a remnant which trusts in the Lord and lives in honesty. They will 'graze and rest', under the benevolent care of the Lord.

Psalm 34 (33) The psalm speaks of the 'humble' and the 'broken-hearted', whom God will heal.

A reading from the holy gospel according to Matthew (21:28-32)

Jesus said to the chief priests and elders of the people: 'What do you think? A man had two sons. Going up to the first he said, "Son, go and work in the vineyard today." He answered, "I will not," but afterwards thought better of it and went. The man then went up to the second and said the same thing, and he answered, "I'll go, sir," but did not go. Which of the two did the father's will?' They said, 'The first.' Jesus said to them, 'Amen I say to you, tax collectors and prostitutes are going into the kingdom of God before you. For John came to you on the road of righteousness, but you did not believe him, and yet the tax collectors and prostitutes did. Even after seeing that, you refused to think better of it and believe in him.'

THIS GOSPEL PASSAGE follows directly after the dispute about 'authority', which was yesterday's gospel reading. Jesus puts a parable to the priests and elders, which once again considers the authority of John the Baptist. They are quick to assert that the son who initially refused and then repented is the better son, and they fall into the trap Jesus has laid for them. He points out that 'tax collectors and prostitutes' responded positively to the preaching of John the Baptist, and to the 'road of righteousness' (*hodos dikaiosunes*) he offered. They were willing to change. Will the priests and elders be able to accept that the parable has a lesson for them?

Why is it so difficult to listen to the words of the gospel? Religious professionals often find it hard to take the risk of faith.

WEDNESDAY OF THE THIRD WEEK IN ADVENT

A reading from the book of Isaiah (45:6-8, 18, 21-25)

There is none but me.
I am the Lord and there is no other;
I form the light and I create darkness,
I make well-being, and I create disaster,
I, the Lord, do all these things.
Drop down dew from above, you heavens,
and let the clouds pour down saving justice,
let the earth open and salvation blossom
and let righteousness spring up with it;
I, the Lord, have created it!
For thus says the Lord, who created the heavens;
he is God, who shaped the earth and set it firm.
He did not create it to be chaos, he formed it to be lived in,
'I am the Lord, and there is no other.
Speak up, present your case, consult together!
Who foretold this in the past,
who declared it long ago?
Was it not I, the Lord?
There is no other god but me,
a righteous God, a saviour, none but me!
Turn to me and you will be saved,
all you ends of the earth,
for I am God and there is no other.
By my own self I swear it;
what comes from my mouth is saving justice,
it is an irrevocable word.
To me every knee shall bend.

By me every tongue shall swear.
Of me it will be said,
"In the Lord alone are saving justice and strength,
until all those who used to rage at him come to him in shame."
In the Lord the whole race of Israel will find saving justice and glory.'

WRITTEN DURING THE exile, the poems in second Isaiah present God in a new way. Most importantly 'I am the Lord, and there is no other.' This is asserted despite the strength of Babylon, and chapter 46 will compare the Lord with the gods of Babylon, who are described as 'cowering'. The God of Israel is also 'creator' (*bara*'): God 'forms' light, 'creates' darkness, 'makes' well-being, 'creates' disaster. The interjection 'drop down dew from above, you heavens, let the clouds pour down saving justice' gives rise to the Advent chant *Rorate caeli desuper*, and is understood as a prayer for the coming of the Messiah. 'Saving justice' and 'righteousness' are also 'created' by the Lord. In the final verses God repeats, 'There is no other god but me', 'a righteous God, a saviour' even for the nations, which are described as 'the ends of the earth'. The Lord, who frees his people, offers them 'saving justice', 'strength' and 'glory'.

Psalm 85 (84) When the Lord comes, 'justice' (*tsedeq*) shall precede him.

A reading from the holy gospel according to Luke (7:19-23)

The disciples of John reported all this to him, and John, summoning two of his disciples, sent them to the Lord to ask, 'Are you the one who is to come, or are we to expect someone else?' When the men reached Jesus they said, 'John the Baptist has sent us to you to ask, "Are you the one who is to come or are we to expect someone else?"' At that time he cured many people of diseases and afflictions and of evil spirits, and gave the gift of sight to many who were blind. And he answered them, 'Go back and tell John what you have seen and heard: the blind see again, the lame walk, lepers are cleansed, and the deaf hear, the dead are raised to life, the good news is proclaimed to the poor; and blessed is anyone who does not find me a cause of stumbling.'

BOTH MATTHEW AND Luke report on the question of John the Baptist which two disciples bring to Jesus. Luke's account is somewhat longer, and emphasises the actual deeds of Jesus 'at that time'. It seems that John, after his imprisonment by Herod the tetrarch, has reflected on the work of Jesus. Perhaps he is struggling with the emphasis on healings, and the welcome offered to sinners. As in Matthew, the words of Jesus end with the beatitude, 'blessed is the one who does not find me a cause of stumbling (*skandalizein*).'

Are you scandalised by the mercy of God?
What God desires is mercy.

THURSDAY OF THE THIRD WEEK IN ADVENT

A reading from the book of Isaiah (54:1-10)

'Shout for joy, you barren one
who has borne no children!
Break into cries of joy, you who were never in labour!
For the children of the forsaken one
outnumber those of the wedded wife,' says the Lord.
'Enlarge the space of your tent,
extend the curtains of your home, do not hold back!
Lengthen your ropes, drive home the tent-pegs,
for you will spread out to the right and to the left;
your descendants will dispossess the nations
and repopulate deserted towns.
Do not fear, you will not be shamed,
do not worry, you will not be disgraced;
for you will forget the shame of your youth
and no longer remember the reproach of your widowhood.
For your creator is your husband,
the Lord Sabaoth is his name;
the Holy One of Israel is your redeemer,
he is called God of all the earth.
For like a wife forsaken and sad at heart,

the Lord has called you back;
like the young wife repudiated, says your God.
I did forsake you for a brief moment,
but in great compassion I shall take you back.
In a flood of anger,
for a moment I hid my face from you
but in everlasting love I have taken pity on you,'
says the Lord, your redeemer.
'This will be to me as it was in the days of Noah
when I swore that Noah's floodwaters
should never again cover the earth.
So now I swear never to be angry with you
and never to rebuke you.
The mountains may depart and the hills may be shaken
but my faithful love will never leave you,
my covenant of peace will never be shaken,'
says the Lord in his pity for you.

THIS TEXT OF Second Isaiah is also found among the readings for the Easter Vigil. It announces the loving mercy of God, who looks on 'the forsaken one'. During Advent it points to the coming of salvation, and at Easter to the fulfilment of this great mystery. God brings to the 'wedded wife' the news that, now that the exile is over, her descendants 'will spread out to the right and to the left'. The identity of the husband is then revealed. He is 'your maker, the Lord Sabaoth, the Holy One of Israel'. His anger is over, and, just as at the end of the story of Noah, 'my faithful love (*hasdi*) will never leave you' and 'my covenant of peace (*berit shelomi)* will never be shaken'. This is the God 'who pities you'.

Psalm 30 (29) The anger of God has passed. Tears turn to joy, and mourning to dancing.

A reading from the holy gospel according to Luke (7:24-30)

When John's messengers had gone Jesus began to talk to the crowds about John, 'What did you go out into the desert to see? A reed swaying in the breeze? Then what did you go out to see? Someone dressed in fine clothes? Look, those who go in magnificent clothes and live luxuriously are to be found at royal courts! Then what did you go out to see? A prophet? Yes, I tell you, and more than a prophet: he is the one of whom it is written:

> *Look, I am going to send my messenger ahead of you to prepare your way before you.*

'I tell you, of the children born to women, no one is greater than John; yet the least in the kingdom of God is greater than he.' All the people who heard him, and the tax collectors too, acknowledged the righteousness of God by accepting baptism from John; but by refusing baptism from him the Pharisees and the lawyers thwarted God's plan for them.

HAVING DELIVERED A veiled criticism of John in the previous verses, which were yesterday's gospel reading, Jesus goes on to praise John. He was 'more than a prophet'. He was the one foretold by Malachi the prophet as 'my messenger' who prepares the way. No one is greater than John, and yet the least in the kingdom is greater. Luke then adds his own comment. By accepting the baptism of John most people 'acknowledged the righteousness of God'; they realised that God was at work in what John did. But the Pharisees and lawyers 'thwarted God's plan for them' by their refusal.

Can you make sense of Jesus' words that the least in the kingdom are greater than John?
Reflect on the person of John the Baptist and his journey of faith, which culminates in martyrdom for the truth.

FRIDAY OF THE THIRD WEEK IN ADVENT

A reading from the book of Isaiah (56:1-3, 6-8)

Thus says the Lord,
'Make fair judgement your concern,
act with justice,

for my salvation is near
and my righteousness is ready to be revealed.
Blessed is anyone who does this,
anyone who holds fast to it, observing the Sabbath,
not profaning it, and holding back from every evil deed.
No foreigner attached to the Lord may say,
"The Lord will firmly exclude me from his people."
As for foreigners who attach themselves to the Lord
to serve him, to love the Lord's name and be his servants,
all who observe the Sabbath, not profaning it,
and hold fast to my covenant:
these I shall lead to my holy mountain
and make them joyful in my house of prayer.
Their burnt offerings and sacrifices on my altar will win my favour,
for my house shall be called a house of prayer for all peoples.'
The Lord God who gathers the exiles of Israel declares,
'There are others I shall gather to him,
besides those already gathered.'

THE FINAL CHAPTERS of the book of Isaiah are produced after the return from exile, and originate from various prophets. This first text from those chapters restates the priorities of 'fair judgement' (*mishpat*) and 'justice' (*tsedaqah*). All those who act accordingly, without exception, are declared 'blessed'. This is then further explained by explicit reference to the 'foreigner', traditionally excluded from temple worship (Deuteronomy 23). The only requirements are respect of the sabbath and of the covenant of the Lord. God will lead them to the 'holy mountain', and 'make them joyful in the house of prayer'. They will be free to offer sacrifices on the altar, for God's house is 'for all peoples' (Mark 11). God's invitation to all is confirmed when God speaks of 'others I shall gather besides those already gathered'. The shepherd God welcomes all (John 10).

Psalm 67 (66) underlines that God's salvation is for all the peoples.

A reading from the holy gospel according to John (5:33-36)

Jesus said to the Jews:
'You sent messengers to John, and he bore witness to the truth.
I do not accept human witness;
it is for your salvation that I say this.
He was the lamp burning and shining
and for a time you were glad to rejoice in his light.
But I have a greater witness than John's:
the deeds my Father has given me to complete,
these same deeds that I do witness that the Father has sent me.'

THE HEALING OF the paralysed man at the pool of Bethsaida in chapter 5 of the Gospel of John has been followed by a debate between Jesus and his interlocutors on the 'work' he does on the Sabbath, and on calling God his 'Father'. At this stage of a long speech Jesus refers to John the Baptist as giving 'witness' (*marturia*) for the truth, a temporary witness who was a 'lamp burning and shining'. But a greater witness claimed by Jesus is provided by the works the Father has given him to complete, and these works bear even stronger testimony that the Father has sent him. Like the gospel readings of the last few days, this final reading of the first period of Advent again mentions the role of John the Baptist.

What 'works of God' provide witness for you in daily life?
A further witness for Jesus in John 5 is the holy Scriptures.

FOURTH SUNDAY OF ADVENT – YEAR A

A reading from the prophet Isaiah (7:10-14)

The Lord spoke to Ahaz again and said:
'Ask the Lord your God for a sign,
either in the depths of Sheol or in the heights above.'
But Ahaz said, 'I will not ask. I will not put the Lord to the test.' He then said:

'Listen now, House of David!
Not satisfied with trying human patience,
will you try my God's patience too?
The Lord will give you a sign in any case.
Look, the virgin is with child
and will give birth to a son
whom she will call Immanuel.'

FOR THE SECOND time in chapter 7 the prophet Isaiah speaks to king Ahaz, who, rather than trusting in God, prefers to play politics with neighbouring nations. Nevertheless, Isaiah tells the king that he will be given a sign from God. The Hebrew text speaks of a 'young woman' ('*almah*), who will give birth to a son. The translation here follows the Greek Bible, which speaks of a 'virgin' (*parthenos*). It is thought that the words of the prophet to the king refer to a son, an heir to the throne, to be born soon. It is not surprising that the text was taken up by the evangelist Matthew and considered fulfilled in the birth of Jesus Christ. The name *Immanuel*, which is the Hebrew for 'God is with us', implies that God is ever faithful to the royal line descended from David.

Psalm 24 (23) tells us that the one 'with clean hands and pure heart' will receive blessing from the Lord.

A reading from the letter of St Paul to the Romans (1:1-7)

From Paul, a servant of Christ Jesus, called to be an apostle, set apart for the gospel that God had promised through his prophets in the holy scriptures, the gospel concerning his Son who, according to the flesh, was a descendant of David and who, in terms of the Spirit and of holiness, was designated Son of God in power by resurrection from the dead: Jesus Christ, our Lord, through whom we have received grace and our apostolic mission of winning the obedience of faith among all the nations for the sake of his name, including yourselves who are called to belong to Jesus Christ. To you all, God's beloved in Rome, called to be saints: grace and peace from God our Father and the Lord Jesus Christ.

THE LETTER TO the Romans, to people whom Paul has not visited but will visit, is arguably the most significant letter of the Apostle Paul. It begins with this long sentence in which Paul describes himself as a 'slave' (*doulos*) of Christ Jesus, 'called to be an apostle', and 'set apart' for the preaching of the gospel. It also gives a full presentation of 'the Son' who is both a descendant of David, and 'Son of God', recognised as such by the resurrection from the dead. It is this Jesus who has commissioned Paul for a mission to announce 'the obedience of faith'. Most importantly, this faith is to be preached to 'all the nations'. In these opening words Paul lays down what is essential in this letter: salvation by faith preached both to the Jews and to the nations.

A reading from the holy gospel according to Matthew (1:18-24)

The birth of Jesus the Messiah happened like this. His mother Mary was betrothed to Joseph; but before they came to live together she was found to be with child through the Holy Spirit. Her husband Joseph, being a righteous man and unwilling to expose her to disgrace, decided to dismiss her quietly. He had this in mind when suddenly an angel of the Lord appeared to him in a dream, saying, 'Joseph, son of David, do not be afraid to take Mary as your wife because the child conceived in her is from the Holy Spirit. She will give birth to a son and you are to name him Jesus, for he will save his people from their sins.' All this took place to fulfil what had been spoken by the Lord through the prophet:

> *Look, the virgin is with child and will give birth to a son, and they shall call his name Emmanuel,*

which means 'God-is-with-us'. When Joseph woke from sleep he did what the angel of the Lord had commanded him and took her as his wife.

MATTHEW'S STORIES OF the birth of Christ are divided into five scenes, of which this is the first. Just as Mary was faced with a decision in Luke 1, so Joseph has to decide whether to take his engaged wife Mary, who is pregnant, to his home. The evangelist makes clear that she is 'with child through the Holy Spirit'. Joseph is described as 'righteous' (*dikaios*), and therefore submissive to the Jewish law, but also unwilling to shame Mary. The appearance of the 'angel of the Lord' speaks of God's invitation in the heart of the human being. Joseph is told that he himself will bestow the child's name, and it will be through him that the legal status of 'son of David' will be established. The evangelist points to the fulfilment of Isaiah 7:14, which he quotes from the Greek translation, intending to indicate by this use of 'virgin' (*parthenos*) the virginal conception of Jesus. The suspense is broken at the end of the passage when we are told that Joseph 'did what the angel of the Lord had commanded him'.

What is the purpose of the fulfilment citations in these chapters of Matthew?

Both Mary and Joseph are invited to make room for God's unexpected ways.

FOURTH SUNDAY OF ADVENT – YEAR B

A reading from the second book of Samuel (7:1-5, 8-12, 14, 16)

Once the king had settled into his house and the Lord had granted him rest from all the enemies surrounding him, the king said to the prophet Nathan, 'Look, I am living in a cedar-wood house, while the ark of God is housed in a tent.' Nathan said to the king, 'Go and do whatever you have in mind, for the Lord is with you.' But that very night, the word of the Lord came to Nathan, 'Go and tell my servant David, "Thus says the Lord, Are you to build me a house for me to live in? I took you from the pasture, from following the sheep, to be leader of my people Israel; I have been with you wherever you went; I have cut off all your enemies for you. I am making your fame as great as the fame of the greatest on earth. I am providing a place for my people Israel; I shall plant them there, and there they will live and never be disturbed again; nor will they be oppressed by the wicked any more, as they were in former times, ever since the time when I instituted judges to govern my people Israel; and I shall grant you rest from all your enemies. The Lord also tells you that he will make you a House.

And when your days are over and you fall asleep with your ancestors, I shall appoint your heir, your own son to succeed you, and I shall make his sovereignty secure. I shall be a father to him and he a son to me; if he does wrong, I shall punish him with a rod such as human beings use, with blows such as humans give. But my faithful love will never be withdrawn from him, as I withdrew it from Saul, whom I removed from before you. Your house and your sovereignty will ever stand firm before me and your throne be for ever secure." '

DAVID HAS ESTABLISHED himself as king in Jerusalem, and tells the prophet Nathan of his plan to build a temple for the Lord, to provide a permanent home for the ark of the covenant, the abiding sign of God's saving presence with Israel. Nathan initially approves of David's plan, but is then told by God to return to the king with the words: 'are you to build me a house (*bayit*) for me to live in?' There are multiple meanings in the Hebrew term: temple, house, royal dynasty. God lists the various ways in which God has supported David, and promises enduring solidarity. It is God who will build the house (*bayit*) of David. God will care for David's descendants too, punishing their offences, but never taking back his 'faithful love' (*hesed*). God will make their 'sovereignty' (*mamlakah*) secure.

Psalm 89 (88) God promises a continuing covenant (*berit*) with David, a dynasty which lasts, and love (*hesed*) which endures.

A reading from the letter of St Paul to the Romans (16:25-27)

And now to him who can make you strong
in accordance with my gospel
and the proclamation of Jesus Christ,
in accordance with the mystery
kept secret for long ages
but now made clear through the writings of the prophets,
and by the command of the eternal God,
made known to all nations,
for the obedience of faith,
to him, the only wise God,

through Jesus Christ
to whom be glory for ever. Amen.

THE LETTER TO the Romans ends with these words, an extensive doxology which acknowledges the gifts of God through Jesus Christ. Paul speaks again of 'my gospel' (*euaggelion*), the Christian 'preaching' (*kerygma*) and the 'mystery' (*mysterion*) which is now revealed. As he had at the beginning of the letter (1:5), he calls for the 'obedience of faith' required of both Jew and Gentile believers. The letter concludes: 'Glory to the only wise God, through Jesus Christ. Amen.'

A reading from the holy gospel according to Luke (1:26-38)

In the sixth month the angel Gabriel was sent by God to a town in Galilee called Nazareth, to a virgin betrothed to a man named Joseph, of the House of David; and the virgin's name was Mary. He went in and said to her, 'Rejoice full of grace! The Lord is with you.' She was deeply disturbed by these words and pondered what this greeting could mean, but the angel said to her, 'Do not be afraid, Mary, for you have found favour with God. Look! You will conceive in your womb and bear a son, and you shall name him Jesus. He will be great and will be called Son of the Most High. The Lord God will give him the throne of his ancestor David; he will rule over the House of Jacob for ever and his reign will have no end.' Mary said to the angel, 'But how can this come about, since I have no knowledge of man?' In answer the angel said to her, 'The Holy Spirit will come upon you, and the power of the Most High will overshadow you. And so the child will be holy and will be called Son of God. And see, your cousin Elizabeth also, in her old age, has conceived a son, and she who was said to be barren is now in her sixth month, *for nothing is impossible to God.*'

Mary said, 'Here I am, the Lord's servant, let it happen to me as you have said.' And the angel left her.

THE 'THRONE OF David' links the gospel of the annunciation to Mary with the words of God to David through the voice of Nathan. Just as Joseph was faced with a choice in the gospel of Matthew, so is Mary of Nazareth in the gospel of Luke. Rather than simply speaking of the 'angel of the Lord' Luke names the 'angel Gabriel', known from the book of Daniel. Gabriel addresses the young girl with the title 'full of grace' (*kecharitomene*), which is derived from the Greek term for 'grace' (*charis*). In Luke's account it is Mary who is to give the name 'Jesus' to her son. Mary's question about how this birth will come about leads to Luke's explanation of a conception by the coming of the Holy Spirit, reminiscent of the explanation given to Joseph in Matthew (1:20). The pregnancy of the elderly Elizabeth is given as a sign to Mary. Mary's answer to the angel ends the suspense when she says: 'let it happen to me as you have said'. The *fiat* of Mary allows the Son of God, the long-awaited Messiah, to be conceived in her womb and to be born into the human race.

How does the annunciation to Mary differ from that to Joseph in Matthew 1?

The name 'Jesus' (yehoshua' / yeshua') means 'the Lord saves'.

FOURTH SUNDAY OF ADVENT – YEAR C

A reading from the prophet Micah (5:1-4)

But you, Bethlehem of Ephrathah,
the least of the clans of Judah,
from you will come for me a future ruler of Israel
whose origin is from the distant past,
from the days of old.
Hence he will abandon them
only until she who is in labour gives birth,
and then those who survive of his race
will be reunited to the Israelites.
He will take his stand and he will shepherd them
in the power of the Lord,
in the majesty of the name of his God,
and they will be secure,
for henceforth his greatness will extend
to the most distant parts of the land.
He himself will be peace!

THE MINOR PROPHET Micah is a contemporary of Isaiah of Jerusalem. While Isaiah promised a royal child in Jerusalem, Micah heralds the birth of a child in David's town of Bethlehem. Both texts are full of hope. For Micah God prefers the humble and the obscure, and the prophet stresses the lowly status of Bethlehem, 'the least of the clans of Judah'. 'Ephrathah' is the clan to which Bethlehem belongs, and is related to the ark of the covenant in Psalm 132. A 'future ruler (*moshel*)' is expected, whose origin is from long ago: he has been long promised. The reference to 'she who is in labour' recalls Isaiah's reference to the young woman with child in chapter 7. Appropriately for a descendant of David, this child will 'shepherd' the sheep, a metaphor frequently used for rulers, most significantly in Ezekiel 34. The people will be 'secure', while the ruler will be 'great', as proclaimed to Mary in Luke 1:32. 'He himself will be peace!' This striking phrase evokes the totality of what the Messiah brings.

Psalm 80 (79) refers to God as 'shepherd of Israel'. It asks God to protect 'the man at your right hand', the anointed king.

A reading from the letter to the Hebrews (10:5-10)

This is what Christ said, on coming into the world:

You wanted no sacrifice or cereal offering,
but you prepared for me a body.
You took no pleasure in burnt offerings or sacrifices for sin;
then I said, 'Here I am, I am coming,'
in the scroll of the book it is written of me,
to do your will, O God.

He says first: *You wanted no sacrifices, cereal offerings, burnt offerings and sacrifices for sin*, and *you took no pleasure* in them – the offerings according to the Law – and then he says: *Here I am! I am coming to do your will.* He is abolishing the first sort to establish the second. And by this *will* we have been made holy through the *offering* of the *body* of Jesus Christ made once and for all.

THE LETTER TO the Hebrews, the great treatise on Christ the high priest, imagines what was in the heart of Christ as he entered the world. He speaks words from Psalm 40: 'you wanted no sacrifices or cereal offerings.' God does not require the sacrifices and offerings of old, but has prepared for Christ a 'body.' The writer takes advantage of the Greek translation of the psalm, which reads 'body' rather than the Hebrew version's 'open ear.' In this body, by his incarnation, Christ comes 'to do the will' of God, which is to accomplish the sanctification of all.

A reading from the holy gospel according to Luke (1:39-45)

Mary set out at that time and went with haste into the hill country to a town in Judah. She went into Zechariah's house and greeted Elizabeth. Now it happened that when Elizabeth heard Mary's greeting, the child leapt in her womb and Elizabeth was filled with the Holy Spirit. She gave a loud cry and said, 'Blessed are you among women, and blessed is the fruit of your womb. Why has this happened to me, that the mother of my Lord should come to me? Look, as soon as your greeting reached my ears, the child in my womb leapt for joy. And, blessed is she who believed that what was said to her from the Lord would be fulfilled.'

MARY MEETS ELIZABETH. Jesus meets John the Baptist. This is an extraordinary story of two encounters. We are not told the words of Mary as she greeted Elizabeth, but instead hear a lengthy speech of Elizabeth, declaring 'blessed' (*eulogemenos*) both Mary and her child, and expressing amazement at the visit. She affirms that the son in her own womb 'leapt for joy.' The evangelist is perhaps alluding to the journey of the ark of the covenant through the 'hill country' of Judah, and David's dancing for joy before the ark (2 Samuel 6:5). The welcome given by David to the ark of God's presence is echoed by the welcome given by John from his mother's womb to the Messiah in the womb of Mary. The final words of Elizabeth, 'blessed (*makaria*) is she who believed' praise Mary for trusting the words delivered to her by the angel, and echo the evangelist Luke's distinct emphasis on 'hearing the word of God and keeping it' (11:28).

How can God be present in the simplicity of the events narrated? God chooses the humble: the shepherd announced by Micah, and Mary of Nazareth.

17th DECEMBER

From December 17th onwards the liturgy provides texts suitable for a more intense preparation. The readings for some of the days of the third week of Advent will not be used in some years, depending on the day of the week on which 17th December falls. The 'O' antiphons, which prepare for Christ with the repeated invocation 'Come!', are sung for the Magnificat at Evening Prayer from 17th to 23rd December. They may be used for the Alleluia verse at Mass on these days, and their full form is provided here with a brief commentary.

A reading from the book of Genesis (49:2, 8-10)

Jacob called his sons and said, 'Gather round and listen, sons of Jacob;
listen to Israel your father.
Judah, your brothers shall praise you:
you grip your enemies by the neck,
your father's sons shall do you homage.
Judah is a lion's whelp;
you stand over your prey, my son.
Like a lion he crouches and lies down,
like a lioness: who dare rouse him?
The sceptre shall not pass from Judah,
nor the ruler's staff from between his feet,
until tribute be brought him
and the peoples render him obedience.

ACCORDING TO THE account in the book of Genesis, as he approaches death Jacob calls his twelve sons and blesses them. Judah, though not the first born, is the most dominant, and in time his name is given to the southern kingdom, which outlives the other tribes. David is of the tribe of Judah, and it is from Judah that the Messiah will come. These blessings, though containing ancient material, also reflect the historical events in which Judah has emerged as the strongest tribe. The bringing of 'tribute' and the rendering of 'obedience' quickly suggested a messianic figure, who would attract all peoples.

Psalm 72 (71), a celebrated messianic psalm, speaks of the Messiah's dominion to the ends of the earth, and the blessings which derive from his rule.

O Antiphon

O Wisdom,
coming from the mouth of the Most High,
ordering all things with strength and gentleness,
come and teach us the way of prudence.

The first of the 'O' antiphons focuses on 'Wisdom' (*Sapientia*). **Sirach 24:3 reads 'I (Wisdom) came from the mouth of the Most High.' Wisdom 8:1 reads: 'Wisdom reaches strongly from one end of the world to the other, and she governs all things well.'**

The beginning of the holy gospel according to Matthew (1:1-17)

Roll of the genealogy of Jesus the Messiah, son of David, son of Abraham:
Abraham was the father of Isaac,
Isaac the father of Jacob,
Jacob the father of Judah and his brothers,
Judah the father of Perez and Zerah, whose mother was Tamar,
Perez the father of Hezron,
Hezron the father of Ram,
Ram the father of Amminadab,
Amminadab the father of Nahshon,
Nahshon the father of Salmon,
Salmon the father of Boaz, whose mother was Rahab,
Boaz the father of Obed, whose mother was Ruth,
Obed the father of Jesse;
and Jesse the father of King David.
David was the father of Solomon, whose mother had been Uriah's wife,
Solomon the father of Rehoboam,
Rehoboam the father of Abijah,

Abijah the father of Asa,
Asa the father of Jehoshaphat,
Jehoshaphat the father of Joram,
Joram the father of Uzziah,
Uzziah the father of Jotham,
Jotham the father of Ahaz,
Ahaz the father of Hezekiah,
Hezekiah the father of Manasseh,
Manasseh the father of Amon,
Amon the father of Josiah;
and Josiah the father of Jechoniah and his brothers.
Then the deportation to Babylon took place.
After the deportation to Babylon,
Jechoniah was the father of Shealtiel,
Shealtiel the father of Zerubbabel,
Zerubbabel the father of Abiud,
Abiud the father of Eliakim,
Eliakim the father of Azor,
Azor the father of Zadok,
Zadok the father of Achim,
Achim the father of Eliud,
Eliud the father of Eleazar,
Eleazar the father of Matthan,
Matthan the father of Jacob,
and Jacob the father of Joseph, the husband of Mary;
of her was born Jesus who is called the Messiah.Therefore all the generations from Abraham to David are fourteen generations, fourteen from David to the Babylonian deportation, and from the Babylonian deportation to the Messiah fourteen generations.

AS WE APPROACH the feast of the birth of the Messiah it is appropriate to rehearse the list of the ancestors. While Luke 3 goes backwards to Adam 'son of God', Matthew 1 moves forwards from Abraham to Jesus, in three sets of fourteen generations. It has been noticed that three times fourteen amounts to six 'sevens', and leaves space for the 'seventh seven', the time of fulfilment and completion, which is brought about by Jesus Christ. In a patriarchal society it is notable to see several women appearing in the genealogy. The ancestral line from Abraham and David reaches Joseph, the 'husband of Mary'. It is Joseph who bestows on Jesus lineage from King David. It is by Mary of course that 'Jesus who is called the Messiah' is born.

Can we rely on the genealogy of Matthew, and if not does it matter?
The Hebrew Bible helps root our lives, past and future, in the goodness of God.

18th DECEMBER

A reading from the prophet Jeremiah (23:5-8)

'Look, the days are coming
declares the Lord–
when I shall raise a righteous Branch for David;
he will reign as king and be wise,
doing what is just and righteous in the land.
In his days Judah will triumph
and Israel live in safety.
And this is the name he will be called:
The-Lord-is-our-Saving-Justice.

'So look, the days are coming – declares the Lord – when people will no longer say, "As the Lord lives who brought the Israelites from the land of Egypt," but, "As the Lord lives who led back and brought home the offspring of the House of Israel from the land of the north and all the lands to which he had driven them, to live in their own land." '

AFTER A HISTORY of poor leadership God announces for the days that are coming the arrival of a 'righteous Branch', a new king of David's line. The emphasis is on what is 'just' (*mishpat*) and 'righteous' (*tsedaqah*). This oracle probably arises during the reign of Zedekiah, whose name means 'The Lord is my justice', but this final king of Judah brought neither justice nor peace. The coming Messiah, however, will establish true justice, and will be worthy of the name 'The Lord is our justice'. In the second part of the reading it is stated that the oath by which the Israelites shall swear will no longer be focussed on God who brought Israel out of Egypt, but on God who regathered the house of Israel from all the lands 'to which he had driven them', in a new act of deliverance which outshines the former exodus.

Psalm 72 (71) The psalm tells us that the true justice brought by the Messiah involves salvation for the poor and needy.

O Antiphon

O Adonai, ruler of the house of Israel,
who appeared to Moses in the burning bush,
and gave the law to him on Sinai,
come and save us with outstretched arm.

The 'O' antiphon is addressed to 'Adonai' (*our Lord*)**, whose name is revealed to Moses from the burning bush (Exodus 3), and who gives the law to him on Sinai (Exodus 20 and 24).**

A reading from the holy gospel according to Matthew (1:18-24)

The birth of Jesus the Messiah happened like this. His mother Mary was betrothed to Joseph; but before they came to live together she was found to be with child through the Holy Spirit. Her husband Joseph, being a righteous man and unwilling to expose her to disgrace, decided to dismiss her quietly. He had this in mind when suddenly an angel of the Lord appeared to him in a dream, saying, 'Joseph, son of David, do not be afraid to take Mary as your wife because the child conceived in her is from the Holy Spirit. She will give birth to a son and you are to name him Jesus, for he will save his people from their sins.' All this took place to fulfil what had been spoken by the Lord through the prophet:

Look, the virgin is with child and will give birth to a son, and they shall call his name Emmanuel, which means 'God-is-with-us'. When Joseph woke from sleep he did what the angel of the Lord had commanded him and took her as his wife.

FOLLOWING THE OPENING genealogy, this is the first of five scenes in the first two chapters of Matthew's gospel which feature the fulfilment of a biblical text. Joseph is the central figure in Matthew's stories, and in this passage he receives a message from an angel, just as Mary will do in the gospel of Luke. Being 'righteous' (*dikaios*), Joseph is committed to the law of God, but also to kindness and generosity. He responds to the strange request of the angel, and thereby to the voice of God, with a willingness which matches that of Mary, his wife. The story is presented as a fulfilment of Isaiah 7:14, which, in the Greek translation, reads: 'the virgin (*parthenos*) is with child and will give birth to a son'. While in the original Hebrew there is no mention of a 'virgin', the Greek text is open to such an interpretation which supports the evangelist's presentation of the virginal conception of Jesus.

Are the servants of the Lord always 'righteous'?
Matthew is particularly keen to demonstrate the fulfilment of Scripture.

19th DECEMBER

A reading from the book of Judges (13:2-7, 24-25)

There was a man of Zorah of the tribe of Dan, called Manoah. His wife was barren; she had borne no children. The angel of the Lord appeared to this woman and said to her, 'You are barren and have had no child, but you shall conceive and bear a son. Now, be careful not to drink wine or fermented liquor, and eat nothing unclean, for you will conceive and bear a son. No razor is to touch his head, for the boy is to be God's nazirite from the womb; and he will begin to rescue Israel from the power of the Philistines.'

The woman then went and told her husband, 'A man of God has just come to me, who looked like the angel of God, so majestic was he. I did not ask him where he came from, and he did not tell me his name. But he said to me, "You shall conceive and bear a son. Now drink no wine or fermented liquor, and eat nothing unclean. For the boy is to be God's nazirite from the womb till the day of his death." '

The woman gave birth to a son and called him Samson. The child grew, and the Lord blessed him; and the spirit of the Lord began to move him.

ANOTHER ANNOUNCEMENT OF the birth of a special child comes in the book of Judges to the wife of Manoah, who is never named. The angel appears first to her, and then on a second occasion when Manoah also speaks with the angel. The instructions about diet first given to the woman are repeated to Manoah. The child, named by his mother as Samson, is to be a 'nazirite', vowed to the Lord from conception until death. This pattern of annunciations of birth in the Hebrew Scriptures is naturally taken up for John the Baptist and for Jesus. The spirit of the Lord will be given to Samson, just as the holy Spirit will fill John the Baptist 'even from his mother's womb' (Luke 1:15). But Samson will use the gift of the Spirit for his own selfish ends.

Psalm 71 (70) speaks of God as a 'rock'. From the womb of the mother God's support and strength is known.

O Antiphon
O root of Jesse,
set up as a sign to the peoples,
kings fall silent before you,
and the peoples acclaim you,
come to save us,
and delay no more.

The great messianic poem speaks of 'a shoot from the root of Jesse' (Isaiah 11:1), father of King David. The spirit of the Lord will rest on him. This 'root' will 'stand as a signal for the peoples' (11:10). Kings fall silent before the servant of the Lord (52:15), and the peoples acclaim him.

A reading from the holy gospel according to Luke (1:5-25)

It happened that in the days of King Herod of Judaea there was a priest called Zechariah who belonged to the Abijah section of the priesthood, and he had a wife, Elizabeth by name, who was a descendant of Aaron. Both were righteous in the sight of God, living blamelessly in all the commandments and observances of the Lord. But they were childless, for Elizabeth was barren and they were both advanced in years.

Now it happened that in the turn of his section to serve, he was exercising his priestly office before God when it fell to him by lot, as the priestly custom was, to enter the Lord's sanctuary and burn incense there. And at the hour of incense all the people were outside, praying.

Then the angel of the Lord appeared to him, standing on the right of the altar of incense. Seeing this, Zechariah was disturbed and overcome with fear. But the angel said to him, 'Do not be afraid, Zechariah, for your prayer has been heard. Your wife Elizabeth is to bear you a son and you shall name him John. You will have joy and delight, and many will rejoice at his birth, for he will be great in the sight of the Lord. He must never drink wine, or strong drink; even from his mother's womb he will be filled with the Holy Spirit, and he will turn many of the Israelites to the Lord their God. With the spirit and power of Elijah, he will go before him *to turn the hearts of fathers to their children* and the disobedient to the wisdom of the righteous, to make ready for the Lord a people prepared for him.' Zechariah said to the angel, '*How can I know this?* I am an old man and my wife is advanced in years.' The angel replied, 'I am Gabriel. I stand in God's presence, and I have been sent to speak to you and bring you this good news. Look! You will be silenced and unable to speak until this has happened, because you did not believe my words, which will come true at their appointed time.' Meanwhile the people were waiting for Zechariah and were surprised that he was delaying in the sanctuary. When he came out he could not speak to them, and they realised that he had seen a vision in the sanctuary. But he could only make signs to them and remained unable to speak.

When his time of service was complete he returned home. After those days his wife Elizabeth conceived and for five months she kept to herself, saying, 'The Lord has done this for me, now that it has pleased him to take away the shame I suffered in public.'

THE NARRATIVE OF the Gospel of Luke begins with the annunciation to Zechariah of the birth of John the Baptist. While the annunciation to Mary takes place in the humble home of Nazareth, this announcement happens in the sanctuary of the temple of Jerusalem. There are obstacles to the fulfilment of God's promise, for Elizabeth is aged and barren. The angel announces that the child is to be named 'John', which means 'the Lord is merciful', and that his rule of life will exclude wine or strong drink. Filled with the Spirit he will assume the power of Elijah, whose return is proclaimed in Malachi 3, to 'make ready for the Lord a people prepared for him'. Zechariah's understandable hesitation is met with the announcement that he is to fall silent, much like the prophet Ezekiel (24:27), until the events come true. The passage ends with the delight of Elizabeth that her 'shame' has been removed through the Lord's gift.

Why does the Lord work in strange and unexpected ways?
The names of John, and of Jesus, make powerful statements about their respective missions.

20th DECEMBER

A reading from the prophet Isaiah (7:10-14)

The Lord spoke to Ahaz again and said:
'Ask the Lord your God for a sign,
either in the depths of Sheol or in the heights above.'
But Ahaz said, 'I will not ask. I will not put the Lord to the test.'
He then said:
'Listen now, House of David!
Not satisfied with trying human patience,
will you try my God's patience too?
The Lord will give you a sign in any case.
Look, the virgin is with child
and will give birth to a son
whom she will call Immanuel.

THIS CELEBRATED MESSIANIC text announces a son and heir for king Ahaz, even though his faith is weak, and he prefers to trust in alien gods rather than in the God of Israel. The 'sign' announced, the birth of a son, guarantees the continuation of the dynasty of David, despite the king's faithlessness. The original Hebrew text uses the word *'almah* , which means 'young woman'. It is the Greek translation which has provided the rendering 'virgin' (*parthenos*). In any case, what is given here is a natural conception of a son for the king. This conception and birth demonstrate God's continuing faithfulness, that 'God is with us', which is the meaning of the Hebrew name '*immanuel*.

Psalm 24(23) The person who 'desires not worthless things' will receive the blessings of the Lord.

O Antiphon

O key of David, sceptre of the House of Israel,
you open and none can close, you close and none can open,
come to free from prison the captive
who lives in darkness and in the shadow of death.

Eliakim receives the key of the palace, so that, as 'father' to the inhabitants of Jerusalem, he may open or close (Isaiah 22:21-22). Apocalypse 3:7 presents Jesus as 'the holy and true one who has the key of David' to open and close.

A reading from the holy gospel according to Luke (1:26-38)

In the sixth month the angel Gabriel was sent by God to a town in Galilee called Nazareth, to a virgin betrothed to a man named Joseph, of the House of David; and the virgin's name was Mary. He went in and said to her, 'Rejoice full of grace! The Lord is with you.' She was deeply disturbed by these words and pondered what this greeting could mean, but the angel said to her, 'Do not be afraid, Mary, for you have found favour with God. Look! You will conceive in your womb and bear a son, and you shall name him Jesus. He will be great and will be called Son of the Most High. The Lord God will give him the throne of his ancestor

David; he will rule over the House of Jacob for ever and his reign will have no end.' Mary said to the angel, 'But how can this come about, since I have no knowledge of man?' In answer the angel said to her, 'The Holy Spirit will come upon you, and the power of the Most High will overshadow you. And so the child will be holy and will be called Son of God. And see, your cousin Elizabeth also, in her old age, has conceived a son, and she who was said to be barren is now in her sixth month, *for nothing is impossible to God.*' Mary said, 'Here I am, the Lord's servant, let it happen to me as you have said.' And the angel left her.

THE ANNUNCIATION STORIES, to Joseph in the gospel of Matthew, and to Zechariah and to Mary in the gospel of Luke, allow the evangelists to proclaim the identity and greatness of the child to be born. While Joseph is told simply that the child he is to call 'Jesus' will 'save his people from their sins', the annunciation to Mary carries an even richer set of statements about Jesus. He will be 'great' and will be called 'Son of the Most High'. He is to receive the throne of 'his ancestor David' and his 'reign will have no end'. While in Matthew's gospel the work of Jesus is summed up in the concept of salvation, here in Luke there are features of the messianic promise given to David in 2 Samuel 7. Mary's question leads to the explanation that she is to conceive 'by the power of the Most High', a daunting revelation which Mary accepts in humility with the words 'Here I am, the Lord's servant, let it happen to me as you have said'.

What might the words 'full of grace' mean?
Both Luke and Matthew are clear that the conception of Jesus is 'from the Holy Spirit' and by 'the power of the Most High'.

21st DECEMBER

A reading from the Song of Songs (2:8-14)

She
The voice of my love!
See how he comes

leaping on the mountains,
bounding over the hills.
My love is like a gazelle,
like a young stag.
See where he stands
behind our wall.
He looks in at the window,
peering through the opening.
My love lifts up his voice,
he says to me:

He
Come then, my love,
my lovely one, come.
For see, winter is past,
the rains are over and gone.
Flowers are appearing on the earth.
The season of songs has come,
the voice of the turtledove is heard in our land.
The fig tree is putting forth its figs
and the blossoming vines give out their fragrance.
Come then, my beloved,
my lovely one, come!
My dove, hiding in the clefts of the rock,
in the coverts of the cliff,
show me your face,
let me hear your voice;
for your voice is sweet
and your face is lovely.

THE SONG OF Songs, a biblical gem, is a celebration of love. First a woman (*She*), and then her lover (*He*), speak in this reading. The woman yearns for the 'beloved' who is coming, and this has been understood also as the yearning of God's people for the Messiah. She envisages him as 'leaping on the mountains', which evokes the story of the Visitation, in which Mary travels through the 'hill country'. In travelling with her child to visit the pregnant Elizabeth she brings about the first meeting of the Lord with the people he loves. The words of the 'beloved' in turn express his longing to meet the woman again, now that 'winter is past', for her 'voice is sweet', and her 'face is lovely', and also suggest the desire of the Messiah to be united with his people, his 'love'. This intimate evocation of love invites a deeper appreciation of human love, and acknowledges the profound yearning to meet the Lord which lies in the human heart, as well as the Lord's longing to meet those he loves.

Alternative first reading

A reading from the prophet Zephaniah (3:14-18)

Shout for joy, daughter Zion,
Israel, shout aloud!
Rejoice, exult with all your heart, daughter Jerusalem!
The Lord has removed your sentence;
he has turned your enemy away.
The Lord is king among you, Israel:
you have nothing more to fear.
On that Day, it will be said to Jerusalem,
'Zion, have no fear, do not let your hands fall limp.'
The Lord your God is within you,
the saving warrior.
He will rejoice over you with gladness,
he will renew you in his love,
he will dance with shouts of joy for you
as on a day of festival.
I have taken away your misfortune,
I no longer need you to bear the disgrace of it.

DELIGHT AT MEETING the loved one is present in this reading too. These words of Zephaniah finish his short book with psalms of joy. It is twice stated that the Lord is 'in your midst'. This is the reason for the rejoicing. The pain of exile and of separation is ended. It is time for dancing, and the Lord will lead the dance. The Lord will renew Israel with his 'love' (*'ahabah*).

Psalm 33 (32) Waiting for the Lord, and the joy of meeting are evoked here.

O Antiphon

O morning star,
radiance of eternal light and sun of justice,
come and enlighten those who live in darkness and in the shadow of death.

Wisdom is described as 'a reflection of the eternal light' (Wisdom 7:26; Hebrews 1:3). Malachi reads: 'for you who revere my name, the sun of justice will rise with healing in his rays' (3:20). The messianic poem in Isaiah 9 speaks of those who dwell 'in shadow dark as death', which is taken up in the *Benedictus* (Luke 1).

A reading from the holy gospel according to Luke (1:39-45)

Mary set out at that time and went with haste into the hill country to a town in Judah. She went into Zechariah's house and greeted Elizabeth. Now it happened that when Elizabeth heard Mary's greeting, the child leapt in her womb and Elizabeth was filled with the Holy Spirit. She gave a loud cry and said, 'Blessed are you among women, and blessed is the fruit of your womb. Why has this happened to me, that the mother of my Lord should come to me? Look, as soon as your greeting reached my ears, the child in my womb leapt for joy. And, blessed is she who believed that what was said to her from the Lord would be fulfilled.'

STRAIGHT AFTER THE annunciations to Zechariah and to Mary in Luke 1 there follows this delightful tale of Mary travelling to visit Elizabeth. The encounter of the two mothers-to-be is also an encounter of their sons in the womb. Elizabeth is the principal speaker here and she reports that as she received Mary's greeting the child in her womb 'leapt for joy'. The child, already 'filled with the holy Spirit' (1:15) from his mother's womb, cannot fail to sense the presence of the Lord. The joy here recalls the rejoicing in the passage from

Zephaniah that 'the Lord is in your midst'. Having expressed her own faith, Elizabeth commends the faith of Mary.

Which is more significant, the meeting of mothers or the meeting of children?
The words of Elizabeth are joined to the words of Gabriel in the 'Hail, Mary'.

22nd DECEMBER

A reading from the first book of Samuel (1:24-28)

When Hannah had weaned Samuel, she took him up with her, as well as a three-year-old bull, an *ephah* of flour and a skin of wine, and took him into the temple of the Lord at Shiloh; the child was very young. They sacrificed the bull and led the child to Eli. She said, 'If you please, my lord! As you live, my lord, I am the woman who stood beside you here, praying to the Lord. This is the child for which I was praying, and the Lord has granted me what I asked of him. Now I make him over to the Lord. For the whole of his life he is made over to the Lord.' Then they worshipped the Lord there.

IN THE TIME of the Judges, before the taking of Jerusalem by David, and the establishment of the temple in that city, Hannah brings her son Samuel, who will be the last of the Judges of Israel, to the temple in Shiloh, the site of an annual pilgrimage feast. Hannah had long been unable to conceive, and had been ridiculed by Peninah, the other wife of their husband Elkanah. Her prayer in the temple had been witnessed by the priest Eli. After the child has been weaned, she comes to present him in the temple, for her prayer has been answered. She 'makes him over to the Lord'. He will stay at Shiloh and serve Eli. In return for her sacrifice, she will be blessed with three more sons and two daughters (1 Samuel 2:21).

1 Samuel 2 The canticle of Hannah contains the words: 'the barren woman bears sevenfold, but the mother of many is left desolate'.

O Antiphon
O king of the nations,
desire of all people,
corner-stone making the two into one,
come and save man,
whom you made from clay.

Jeremiah 10:7 heralds the Lord as 'king of the nations'. 'Desire of all peoples' is a phrase found in the Latin Vulgate of Haggai 2:8. Isaiah speaks of a 'precious corner-stone' (28:16), and Psalm 118:22 of 'a stone rejected which becomes the corner stone'. Making 'the two into one' is the role of the Messiah in Ephesians 2:14. And 'moulded from clay' takes us back to the origins of human beings according to Genesis 2:7.

A reading from the holy gospel according to Luke (1:46-56)

And Mary said:
'My soul proclaims the greatness of the Lord
and my spirit *rejoices in God my Saviour*;
since *he has looked with favour on the lowliness of his servant.*
For see, from now on all generations will call me blessed,
for the Almighty has done great things for me.
and *holy is his name,*
and *his mercy is from generation to generation on those who fear him.*
He has exerted the power of his arm,
he has scattered the proud in the thoughts of their heart.
He has taken down princes from thrones *and raised up the lowly.*
He has filled the hungry with good things, and sent the rich away empty.
He has come to the help of Israel his servant,
in remembrance of his mercy,
according to the promise he made to our ancestors,

of his mercy to Abraham and his descendants for ever.'
Mary stayed with Elizabeth some three months and then went back home.

THIS PRAYER OF praise and thanksgiving placed on the lips of Mary by the evangelist is the prayer of the church every evening at Evening Prayer. The personal thanksgiving in the opening verses for the 'great things' the Lord has done 'for me' is transformed into an extended eulogy of the 'mercy' (*eleos*) of God shown 'to those who fear him' over the generations. God's intervention in favour of the lowly and the hungry contrasts with his rejection of the proud, the princes and the rich. The final focus is on God's deeds for Israel 'his servant', according to the promise made of 'mercy' (*eleos*) to Abraham and his descendants. The concluding statement that Mary remained with Elizabeth 'some three months' hints that she remained until the birth of John.

How central is mercy to the message of the gospel?
The Magnificat is modelled on the prayer of Hannah in 1 Samuel 2.

23rd DECEMBER

A reading from the prophet Malachi (3:1-4, 23-24)

'Look, I am sending my messenger to prepare the way before me. And suddenly the Lord whom you seek will come to his Temple; yes, the angel of the covenant in whom you delight is on his way, says the Lord Sabaoth. Who can endure the day of his coming? Who will remain standing when he appears? For he is like a refiner's fire, like fullers' alkali. He will take his seat as refiner and purifier; he will purify the sons of Levi and refine them like gold and silver so that they can make the offering to the Lord in righteousness. The offering of Judah and Jerusalem will then be acceptable to the Lord as in former days, as in the former years.

'Look, I shall send you the prophet Elijah before the great and awesome Day of the Lord comes. He will turn the hearts of parents to their children and of children to their parents so that I shall not strike the land with a curse of destruction.'

THE THIRD CHAPTER of the minor prophet Malachi begins with another reference to 'my messenger' (*mal'aki*), the anonymous prophet to whom the book is attributed. This prophet speaks of the coming of the Lord, described also as 'the angel (*mal'ak*) of the covenant'. He will reestablish the covenant by his work of purification. It is the 'sons of Levi', the priestly groups, who most of all stand in need of renewal, so that they can once again make their offerings in 'righteousness' (*tsedaqah*), as in the days before the exile. The final two verses are the last verses of the book of Malachi and are likely to be an addition. It speaks about the return of the prophet Elijah 'before the great and awesome Day of the Lord'. His role is to bring about reconciliation. In this way the 'curse of destruction' (*herem*) will be avoided.

Psalm 25 (24) Once again the Lord intervenes and 'shows the path to those who stray'.

O Antiphon

O Emmanuel,
our king and lawgiver,
hope of the nations and their saviour,
come and save us, Lord our God.

This final 'O' antiphon takes up Isaiah 7:14: the child to be born of the 'young woman' ('*almah*) is to be called 'God is with us' ('*immanuel*). Isaiah 33:22 proclaims: 'The Lord is our king, he will save us.' Zechariah also speaks of the coming 'king', 'righteous' and 'victorious'. The Servant of the Lord is made 'a light to the nations' and brings salvation to the ends of the earth (Isaiah 49:6).

A reading from the holy gospel according to Luke (1:57-66)

The time came for Elizabeth to give birth, and she gave birth to a son; and her neighbours and relations heard that the Lord had lavished his mercy on her, and they shared her joy.

Now it happened that on the eighth day they came to circumcise the child; they were going to call him Zechariah after his father, but his mother spoke up, saying, 'No, he shall be called John.' They said to her, 'But no one in your family has that name,' and made signs to his father to find out what he wanted him called. The father asked for a writing-tablet and wrote, 'His name is John.' And they were all astonished. Immediately his mouth was opened and his tongue freed and he began to speak praising God. Fear came over all their neighbours, and the whole affair was talked about throughout the hill country of Judaea. All those who heard of it took it to heart, saying, 'What then is this child to be?' And indeed the hand of the Lord was with him.

THE REPORT OF the birth of John is brief, and her 'neighbours and relations' acknowledge the great 'mercy' (*eleos*) of God shown to Elizabeth. The eighth day is the day of circumcision and naming, and it is the naming that commands attention. Before being struck dumb Zechariah had been told that the name of the child was to be 'John' (*Ioannes*) (1:13). But now it is his mother who, in the absence of words from his father, maintains that his name is to be 'John', despite the fact that 'no one in your family has that name'. The father writes 'His name is John', and his speech returns. The giving of a new name, which means 'God is merciful' (*yehohanan*), is a sign of a new time of forgiveness and hope, and a clear message of mercy from God. It is no surprise that the word 'mercy' (*eleos*) is found twice in each of the two canticles which bracket this story (1:50,54 and 1:72,78). The extraordinary events at the circumcision of John raise the question from all those who 'took it to heart' saying 'What is this child to be?'

What is Luke's purpose in giving such details about John?
Luke gives far more space to the naming than to the actual birth of John.

24th DECEMBER (morning)

A reading from the second book of Samuel (7:1-5, 8-12, 14-16)

Once the king had settled into his house and the Lord had granted him rest from all the enemies surrounding him, the king said to the prophet Nathan, 'Look, I am living in a cedar-wood house, while the ark of God is housed in a tent.' Nathan said to the king, 'Go and do whatever you have in mind, for the Lord is with you.' But that very night, the word of the Lord came to Nathan, 'Go and tell my servant David, "Thus says the Lord, Are you to build me a house for me to live in? I took you from the pasture, from following the sheep, to be leader of my people Israel; I have been with you wherever you went; I have cut off all your enemies for you. I am making your fame as great as the fame of the greatest on earth. I am providing a place for my people Israel; I shall plant them there, and there they will live and never be disturbed again; nor will they be oppressed by the wicked any more, as they were in former times, ever since the time when I instituted judges to govern my people Israel; and I shall grant you rest from all your enemies. The Lord also tells you that he will make you a House. And when your days are over and you fall asleep with your ancestors, I shall appoint your heir, your own son to succeed you, and I shall make his sovereignty secure. I shall be a father to him and he a son to me. Your house and your sovereignty will ever stand firm before me and your throne be for ever secure."'

THE DECISION OF David to build a 'house' (*bayit*) for the Lord is the context for a long speech of the Lord transmitted by the prophet Nathan. No clear reason is given why David should not build the temple, except that it is God who builds him a house. The promise of God's solidarity extends to David's son, Solomon, who will indeed build a temple, but the text is quickly understood as a foundation for the messianic promise.

Psalm 89 (88) The Lord makes a covenant with David, his servant (*'ebed*), and promises his enduring love (*hesed*).

A reading from the holy gospel according to Luke (1:67-79)

Zechariah was filled with the Holy Spirit and spoke this prophecy:

Blessed be the Lord, the God of Israel,
for he has looked favourably on his people and *set them free*,
and he has established for us a saving power

in the House of his servant David,
just as he spoke by the mouth of his holy prophets from of old,
salvation from our *enemies* and *from the hands of all who hate us*,
to show *mercy to our ancestors*,
and *remember his* holy *covenant*,
the oath he swore to our father Abraham,
to grant us, free from fear, delivered from the hands of our enemies,
to serve him in holiness and righteousness
in his presence, all our days.
And you, child, shall be called prophet of the Most High,
for you will go before *the Lord*
to prepare his ways,
to give his people knowledge of salvation
by forgiveness of their sins,
by the heartfelt mercy of our God
by which the dawn from on high will visit us,
to give light to *those who live*
in darkness and the shadow of death,
and to guide our feet into
the way of peace.'

THIS FINAL GOSPEL of Advent is appropriately a song of thanksgiving, the *Benedictus*, which is prayed at Morning Prayer throughout the church. Zechariah provides words for God's people to acknowledge that God has 'looked favourably on his people and set them free'. The 'saving power', literally 'horn of salvation' (*keras soterias*), is clearly a reference to the coming Saviour. God has demonstrated mercy (*eleos*) to the ancestors in the past, but a new deed is being prepared. Specifically, Zechariah thanks God for his child John and for his mission of going before the Lord 'to prepare his ways' (Isaiah 40:3). The 'dawn from on high' (*anatole ex hupsous*) will visit God's people, bringing light to those 'in darkness and the shadow of death' (Isaiah 9:1), and guiding our feet 'into the way of peace'.

How do the two canticles invite our response to the Advent readings? We stand now on the brink of the fulfilment of all God's promises.

CHRISTMAS READINGS

CHRISTMAS VIGIL MASS

A reading from the prophet Isaiah (62:1-5)

About Zion I will not be silent,
about Jerusalem I will not be quiet,
until saving justice comes forth for her like a dawning light
and her salvation burns up like a torch.
The nations will see your saving justice
and all kings your glory
and you will be called a new name
which the mouth of the Lord will bestow.
You will be a crown of splendour
in the hand of the Lord,
a royal diadem in the hand of your God.
No more will you be known as 'Forsaken'
or your land be termed 'Desolate';
but you will be called 'My Delight is in her'
and your land 'The Espoused';
for the Lord will take delight in you
and your land shall be espoused.
Like a young man marrying a virgin,
your rebuilder shall wed you
and as the bridegroom rejoices in his bride,
so will your God rejoice in you.

THE FIRST READING of Christmas brings an explosion of joy and light. 'Saving justice' (*tsedeq*) in Jerusalem will be like the dawn, and 'salvation' (*yeshu'ah*) like a torch. In post-exilic times it is still awaited, both by Israel and by the nations. New treasures will be awarded, a 'crown of splendour', a 'royal diadem', and new names will be bestowed, no longer 'forsaken', or 'desolate', but 'my delight in her' (*hephtsi-bah*) and 'espoused' (*be'ulah*). The Lord delights in marriage to his bride, Jerusalem. God rejoicing in his people suggests the joy of the coming of the Messiah, who rejoices to be among the children of God.

Psalm 89 (88) People find their joy in the name of the Messiah, and adopt his ways of justice.

A reading from the Acts of the Apostles (13:16-17, 22-25)

So Paul stood up, raised his hand for silence and began to speak:

'Men of Israel, and God-fearers, listen! The God of this people Israel chose our ancestors and exalted our people during their stay in Egypt, and with uplifted arm led them out from there. He raised up David as a king for them, whom he attested in these words, "*I have found David* son of Jesse, *a man after my own heart, who will perform my entire will.*" From this man's posterity, according to his promise, he brought to Israel a saviour, Jesus, whose coming was heralded by John, proclaiming a baptism of repentance to the whole people of Israel. As John was finishing his course he said, 'Who do you think I am? I am not he. Look! One is coming after me, the strap of whose sandal I am not worthy to undo."'

DURING HIS FIRST missionary journey Paul is invited to speak in the synagogue of Antioch in Pisidia. Paul and Barnabas have been asked for a 'word of consolation', and they announce the good news. The reading offers some early verses of Paul's long speech, which reaches its climax with the Christian *kerygma* of the death and resurrection of Jesus. In the verses read at this Christmas Mass Paul proclaims that from David's 'posterity' (*sperma*), and 'according to the promise' (*epaggelia*), a saviour has been born, and that John the Baptist proclaimed 'a baptism of repentance', and pointed to the 'one who is coming after me'.

The beginning of the holy gospel according to Matthew (1:1-25)

Roll of the genealogy of Jesus the Messiah, son of David, son of Abraham:

Abraham was the father of Isaac,
Isaac the father of Jacob,
Jacob the father of Judah and his brothers,

Judah the father of Perez and Zerah, whose mother was Tamar,
Perez the father of Hezron,
Hezron the father of Ram,
Ram the father of Amminadab,
Amminadab the father of Nahshon,
Nahshon the father of Salmon,
Salmon the father of Boaz, whose mother was Rahab,
Boaz the father of Obed, whose mother was Ruth,
Obed the father of Jesse;
and Jesse the father of King David.
David was the father of Solomon, whose mother had been Uriah's wife,
Solomon the father of Rehoboam,
Rehoboam the father of Abijah,
Abijah the father of Asa,
Asa the father of Jehoshaphat,
Jehoshaphat the father of Joram,
Joram the father of Uzziah,
Uzziah the father of Jotham,
Jotham the father of Ahaz,
Ahaz the father of Hezekiah,
Hezekiah the father of Manasseh,
Manasseh the father of Amon,
Amon the father of Josiah;
and Josiah the father of Jechoniah and his brothers.
Then the deportation to Babylon took place.
After the deportation to Babylon,
Jechoniah was the father of Shealtiel,
Shealtiel the father of Zerubbabel,
Zerubbabel the father of Abiud,
Abiud the father of Eliakim,
Eliakim the father of Azor,
Azor the father of Zadok,
Zadok the father of Achim,
Achim the father of Eliud,
Eliud the father of Eleazar,
Eleazar the father of Matthan,
Matthan the father of Jacob,

and Jacob the father of Joseph, the husband of Mary;
of her was born Jesus who is called the Messiah.

Therefore all the generations from Abraham to David are fourteen generations, fourteen from David to the Babylonian deportation, and from the Babylonian deportation to the Messiah fourteen generations. The birth of Jesus the Messiah happened like this. His mother Mary was betrothed to Joseph; but before they came to live together she was found to be with child through the Holy Spirit. Her husband Joseph, being a righteous man and unwilling to expose her to disgrace, decided to dismiss her quietly. He had this in mind when suddenly an angel of the Lord appeared to him in a dream, saying, 'Joseph, son of David, do not be afraid to take Mary as your wife because the child conceived in her is from the Holy Spirit. She will give birth to a son and you are to name him Jesus, for he will save his people from their sins.' All this took place to fulfil what had been spoken by the Lord through the prophet:

> *Look, the virgin is with child and will give birth to a son, and they shall call his name Emmanuel,*

which means 'God-is-with-us'. When Joseph woke from sleep he did what the angel of the Lord had commanded him and took her as his wife. He had not had intercourse with her when she gave birth to a son, and he named him Jesus.

MATTHEW CAREFULLY BEGINS his gospel by placing 'Jesus, who is called the Messiah' at the climax of the generations descended from Abraham and David. Three sets of fourteen generations amount to six 'sevens', and the 'seventh seven', the time of fulfilment, will be the new time brought by Christ. Having completed the genealogy, the evangelist tells us 'how' Jesus the Messiah came to be born. The focus is on Joseph and his willingness to care for the child and his mother, and his crucial role in naming him 'Jesus', the one who is to 'save' his people. It is through Joseph that the Davidic heritage of Jesus is established. Matthew demonstrates the fulfilment in these events by quoting from the prophet Isaiah, the first of a multitude of quotations from the scriptures in his gospel.

Do I have the imagination to accept that God's plans are different? Both Mary and Joseph were ready for the unexpected.

CHRISTMAS NIGHT MASS

A reading from the prophet Isaiah (9:1-6)

The people that walked in darkness have seen a great light;
on the inhabitants of a country in shadow dark as death,
light has blazed forth.
You have enlarged the nation,
you have increased its joy;
they rejoice before you as people rejoice at harvest time,
as they exult when they are dividing plunder.
For the yoke that weighed on them,
the bar across their shoulders,
the rod of their oppressor,
these you have broken as on the day of Midian.
For all the footgear clanking over the ground
and all the clothing rolled in blood
will be burnt, will be food for the flames.
For a son has been born for us,
a son has been given to us
and dominion has been laid on his shoulders;
and this is the name he has been given,
'Wonder-Counsellor, Mighty-God, Eternal-Father, Prince-of-Peace'.
His rule will be great and there will be no end of peace
for the throne of David and his kingdom,
secure and established in fair judgement and righteousness.
From this time onwards and for ever
the jealous love of the Lord Sabaoth will do this.

IN THE DEEPEST darkness of night this messianic poem of the prophet Isaiah invites us to embrace the light of Christ. God has saved his people and brought them rejoicing. This is compared to the rejoicing of harvest time, and of sharing the spoils of war. Three specific reasons for rejoicing are then given: an end to oppression, an end to war, and the birth of a child. The context may well be the enduring Assyrian threat. The birth of the child signifies, as in Isaiah 7:14, that God's solidarity continues, that 'God is with us'. The names are such as are given at the coronation of a prince, and conclude with 'Prince-of-

Peace'. Such a list of titles is given to David in 2 Samuel 23, and the poem ends with the promise of an enduring kingdom, as had been made to David through Nathan the prophet (2 Samuel 7).

Psalm 96 (95) contains an invitation to all peoples to sing a 'new song', which is enhanced by the rejoicing of all creation.

A reading from the letter of St Paul to Titus (2:11-14)

The grace of God our Saviour has been revealed to the whole human race, teaching us that, giving up impiety and all worldly passions, we should be self-restrained and live righteous and religious lives in this present world, waiting for the blessed hope and the appearing of the glory of our great God and Saviour Christ Jesus. He offered himself for us in order to ransom us from all our faults and to purify a people to be his very own, eager to do good.

THE LETTER TO Titus speaks of the 'revealing' (*epiphainein)* of the 'grace' (*charis*) of God for the salvation of all. God invites 'the whole human race' to live 'righteous and religious lives'. They should await the 'blessed hope' (*he makaria elpis*) , the 'appearing' (*epiphaneia*) of the 'glory' (*doxa*) 'of our great God and of our Saviour Jesus Christ'. The essence of Christ's work is then resumed in that he 'offered himself' so as to 'ransom' (*lytroun*) and 'purify' (*katharizein)* a people to be his own. The free gift of grace encourages people to live lives full of good works.

A reading from the holy gospel according to Luke (2:1-14)

Now it happened that at this time a decree came out from Caesar Augustus that a register should be made of the whole world. This registration – the first – took place while Quirinius was governor of Syria, and everyone went to be registered, each to his own town. So Joseph set out from the town of Nazareth in Galilee for Judaea, to David's town called Bethlehem, since he was of David's House and line, in order to be registered together with Mary, his betrothed, who was with child. Now it happened that, while they were there, the time came for her to have her child, and she gave birth to her son, the first-born. She wrapped him in swaddling clothes and laid him in a manger, because there was no room for them in the living-space. In that countryside there were shepherds living in the fields keeping the night watch over their flock. An angel of the Lord stood over them and the glory of the Lord shone round them. They were terrified, but the angel said, 'Do not be afraid. Look, I bring you good news of great joy for the whole people, that today a Saviour has been born to you in the town of David, who is Christ the Lord. And this is a sign for you: you will find a baby wrapped in swaddling clothes and lying in a manger.' And suddenly there was with the angel a throng of the heavenly host, praising God and saying:

'Glory to God in the highest heaven,
and on earth peace among people of good will.'

THAT JOSEPH WAS descended from King David was announced in the account of the annunciation to Mary (Luke 1:27), and by the angel to Joseph 'son of David' in the Gospel of Matthew (Matthew 1:20). His davidic descent is affirmed again here with the statement that Mary and Joseph were forced to travel to Bethlehem by the 'decree' (*dogma*) of the emperor Caesar Augustus, so that Joseph could be registered in David's town. Luke thus relates the coming birth to the history of Israel and places it within the context of the Roman occupation of Palestine. The birth of the child is into straightened circumstances, so that the newborn is laid to rest in a manger (*phatne*), a feeding trough for animals. The first visitors to the newborn child are shepherds, a deprived and despised social group. To such people the 'angel of the Lord' brings 'good news' (*euaggelizein*) of the birth of the Messiah. Luke's point that Jesus has come to 'preach good news to the poor' (Luke 4) is thus affirmed from the very beginning. Luke celebrates the birth of the Messiah with an angelic throng heralding peace on earth.

How realistic is this account of the birth of Jesus?
The one who is 'son' of God is born into deprivation and oppression.

CHRISTMAS DAWN MASS

A reading from the prophet Isaiah (62:11-12)

See, the Lord has proclaimed to the end of the earth:
say to the daughter Zion,
'See, your salvation is coming.
See, his reward is with him,
his achievement precedes him!'
They shall be called 'the Holy People', 'the redeemed of the Lord',
and you yourself shall be called 'Sought-out', 'City-not-forsaken'.

THE BRIEFEST OF the Christmas readings is dominated by a triple initial 'See!' translated from the Hebrew *hinneh*, which is often rendered with the archaic 'behold!' The message, to be brought to the 'end of the earth', concerns 'the daughter Zion' who is told that 'salvation', deliverance, liberation (*yesha'*), is close at hand. This is all we need to hear. The Lord's 'reward' (40:10) is not booty or riches but his people, and, to confirm that what they are living is real, they will be renamed as 'holy', as 'redeemed' (*ge'ullim*). God has indeed ransomed them, for the exile is ended. They are 'sought out' and 'not forsaken'. God's eternal solidarity with suffering people is spelt out.

Psalm 97 (96) The psalm tells how light shines for the just one (*tsaddiq*), and for the 'upright of heart'.

A reading from the letter of St Paul to Titus (3:4-7)

When the kindness and love of God our Saviour for humanity were revealed, not because of any works of righteousness we had ourselves done but in accordance with his own mercy, he saved us through the washing of rebirth and renewal in the Holy Spirit which he generously poured over us through Jesus Christ our Saviour so that, justified by his grace, we should become heirs in hope of eternal life.

AS IN THE reading from this letter read at the Mass in the Night (2:11), we hear of a revelation. This time the 'kindness' (*chrestotes*) and 'love', love of humanity (*philanthropia*), of 'God our Saviour' are 'revealed' (*epiphainein*). It is stressed that this is not due to any works 'of justice' we have performed, but entirely a gift of the 'mercy' (*eleos*) of God. Our salvation comes through the 'washing of rebirth' (*paliggenesia*), our baptism, and through 'renewal' (*anakainosis*) in the Holy Spirit. We are thus 'born again' in the Spirit. The feast of Christmas reveals the trinitarian free gift of God through Christ 'the Saviour' in the Holy Spirit. We are 'justified by the grace' of God, becoming 'heirs' to the hope of eternal life.

A reading from the holy gospel according to Luke (2:15-20)

Now it happened that when the angels had gone from them into heaven, the shepherds said to one another, 'Let us go now to Bethlehem and see this event which the Lord has made known to us.' So they went in haste and found Mary and Joseph, and the baby lying in the manger. When they saw this, they made known what they had been told about this child, and everyone who heard it was astonished at what the shepherds said to them. But Mary treasured all these things and pondered them in her heart. And the shepherds went back glorifying and praising God for all they had heard and seen, just as they had been told.

THE SHEPHERDS READILY comply with the instruction from the Lord given by the angel and go to witness this 'event' (*pema*). There is a simple acknowledgement of what they see: Mary and Joseph and the child in the manger. The focus of these verses is on the reactions of the shepherds and of Mary. While the shepherds 'make known' the word (*pema*) they have been told, so that everyone is astonished, Mary does not speak and simply ponders 'all these things' (*pemata*) in her heart. The shepherds' witness continues as they return to their flocks 'glorifying and praising God'. It is stressed that what they had seen was 'just as they had been told'. Word and event coincide.

The role of the shepherds is to pass on the 'good news' brought to them. The silence of Mary speaks louder than words.

CHRISTMAS DAY MASS

A reading from the prophet Isaiah (52:7-10)

How lovely on the mountains
are the feet of the messenger announcing peace,
of the messenger of good news, proclaiming salvation
and saying to Zion, 'Your God is king!'
Your watchmen raise their voices,
shouting for joy together,
for with their own eyes
they have seen the Lord returning to Zion.
Break into shouts of joy together,
you ruins of Jerusalem;
for the Lord has had mercy on his people,
he has redeemed Jerusalem.
The Lord has bared his holy arm
in the sight of all nations,
and all the ends of the earth
have seen the salvation of our God.

THIS POEM TAKES up the themes with which the second Isaiah began in chapter 40. A messenger brings to Sion news of peace (*shalom*), good news of salvation (*tob*), declaring the reign of God. Watchmen witness the return of the Lord to Sion. The words of comfort with which this prophet began to speak are reiterated: 'the Lord has comforted (*naham*) his people' (40:1) and 'redeemed Jerusalem'. Exile is at an end, and all nations, the 'ends of the earth', have 'seen the salvation of our God'.

Psalm 98 (97) Like the prophet, this psalmist speaks of the 'holy arm' of God bringing salvation to the nations.

A reading from the letter to the Hebrews (1:1-6)

In many ways and by many means in the past, God spoke to our ancestors through the prophets, but in these last days he has spoken to us in his Son, whom he appointed heir of all things and through whom he made the ages. He is the reflection of God's glory and the imprint of God's own being, sustaining all things by his powerful word. Now that he has made purification for sins, he has taken his seat at the right hand of the Majesty on high. So he is now far above the angels, as the name which he has inherited is more excellent than theirs.

For to which of the angels has God ever said:

You are my Son, today I have fathered you,

or:

I shall be as a father to him and he as a son to me?

Again, when he brings the First-born into the world, he says:

Let all the angels of God worship him.

IN THE COMING of the Messiah God speaks a new word to the world. God has spoken in many and various ways through the prophets, but now God speaks through the Son, 'heir' of all things, and creator of all. The Son is the 'reflection' (*apaugasma*) of God's glory, and 'imprint' (*charakter*) of God's very being. He comes to 'make purification for sin'. The Letter to the Hebrews will develop this thought by speaking of the sacrifice made 'once and for all' (*ephapax*) (7:27) by Christ, the 'high priest' (2:17) of the new covenant. The incarnate Son, originating above the angels, lowers himself even to death, and is then exalted 'far above the angels'.

The beginning of the holy gospel according to John (1:1-18)

In the beginning was the Word:
the Word was with God
and the Word was God.
He was with God in the beginning.
Through him all things came into being,
not one thing came into being except through him.
What has come into being in him was life,
life that was the light of all people;

and light shines in darkness,
and darkness could not overpower it.
There was a man sent by God.
His name was John.
He came as a witness,
to bear witness to the light,
so that everyone might believe through him.
He was not the light,
he was to bear witness to the light.
The true light
that gives light to everyone
was coming into the world.
He was in the world
and the world came into being through him,
and the world did not know him.
He came to what was his own
and his own people did not accept him.
But to those who did accept him
he gave power to become children of God,
to those who believed in his name,
who were born not from blood,
or from the will of the flesh,
or from human will
but from God himself.
The Word became flesh,
and lived among us,
and we saw his glory,
the glory as of an only-begotten Son of the Father,
full of grace and truth.
John witnesses to him and cried out, saying,
'This is the one of whom I said:
He who comes after me
has passed ahead of me
because he was before me.'
Indeed, from his fullness
we have all received,
grace upon grace,

for the Law was given through Moses,
grace and truth came through Jesus Christ.
No one has ever seen God;
it is the only-begotten Son,
who is close to the Father's heart,
who has made him known.

THE OPENING VERSES of the Fourth Gospel speak of the incarnation of the Word, inviting us to penetrate to the fundamental truth of the Christmas mystery. John deliberately begins his gospel with the words 'in the beginning' (*en arche*), echoing the book of Genesis, for this is a new beginning for creation. The Word (*logos*), who was with God in the beginning and through whom everything was made, is the light (*phos*) coming into the world. The Baptist bears witness. While there are those who do not accept him, those who believe in his name are reborn. The Word 'became flesh' (*sarx*), and lived among us so that we could see his 'glory' (*doxa*), which is full of 'grace' (*charis*) and 'truth' (*aletheia*). He brings 'grace upon grace'. He makes the invisible God known (*exegeisthai*).

How does Christological teaching connect with the birth in the manger?
The humanity of the Son of God is the culmination of the love of the Father.

SUNDAY IN THE CHRISTMAS OCTAVE – FEAST OF THE HOLY FAMILY – YEAR A

A reading from the book of Ecclesiasticus (3:2-6, 12-14)

The Lord honours the father above his children
and upholds the rights of a mother over her children.
Whoever respects a father atones for sins,
whoever honours a mother is like someone amassing a fortune.
Whoever respects a father will have joy in children

and will be heard at the time of prayer.
Long life comes to anyone who honours a father;
whoever obeys the Lord makes a mother happy.
My child, support your father in his old age,
do not grieve him as long as he lives.
Even if his mind should fail, show him sympathy;
in your full strength do not dishonour him;
for kindness to a father will not be forgotten
but will serve as reparation for your sins.

THE WISDOM OF Ben Sira, contained in the book of Ecclesiasticus, presents a wealth of moral teaching. The material in this reading might be seen as a commentary on the commandment: 'Honour your father and your mother so that you may live long in the land that the Lord your God is giving you.' (Exodus 20:12) Ben Sira spells out some consequences of fidelity to this commandment. In particular honour paid to a father leads to 'long life'. The consideration to be shown to an elderly father, and the invitation to 'sympathy' if 'his mind should fail' are ever relevant.

Psalm 128 (127) The psalm lists the blessings of family.

A reading from the letter of St Paul to the Colossians (3:12-21)

As the chosen of God, then, holy and beloved, clothe yourselves in heartfelt compassion, in generosity and humility, gentleness and patience. Bear with one another; forgive one another if anyone has a complaint against another. Just as the Lord has forgiven you, so must you do the same. Over all these, put on love, the bond of perfection. And may the peace of Christ reign in your hearts, to which indeed you were called in one body. Always be grateful. Let the word of Christ dwell in you richly. Teach and advise one another in all wisdom. With gratitude sing psalms and hymns and inspired songs to God in your hearts; and whatever you say or do, do everything in the name of the Lord Jesus, giving thanks to God the Father through him.

Wives, be subject to your husbands, as is fitting in the Lord.

Husbands, love your wives and do not be sharp with them. Children, be obedient to your parents always, for that is pleasing to the Lord. Parents, do not provoke your children so that they do not lose heart.

AWARENESS OF BEING 'chosen' and being 'forgiven' is strong motivation for Christian conduct. The various virtues listed are compared to clothing, and over all these the Christian should 'put on love' (*agape*), which is described as 'the bond of perfection'. General exhortations that 'the peace of Christ' should 'reign in your hearts' and that 'the word of Christ' should 'dwell in you richly' are followed by invitations to gratitude. The passage concludes with specific advice to 'wives', 'husbands', 'children' and 'parents', and the contemporary convention that wives should 'be subject' to husbands is not challenged.

A reading from the holy gospel according to Matthew (2:13-15, 19-23)

After the wise men had left, see, an angel of the Lord appeared to Joseph in a dream and said, 'Get up. Take the child and his mother, flee into Egypt and stay there until I tell you, for Herod intends to search for the child to destroy him.' So Joseph got up and, taking the child and his mother by night, left for Egypt and stayed there until the death of Herod. This was to fulfil what had been spoken by the Lord through the prophet, saying:

I called my son out of Egypt.

When Herod had died, see, an angel of the Lord appeared in a dream to Joseph in Egypt saying, 'Get up. Take the child and his mother and go to the land of Israel, for those who were seeking the child's life are dead.' So Joseph got up and, taking the child and his mother, went to the land of Israel. But when he learnt that Archelaus was king of Judaea in place of his father, Herod, he was afraid to go there, and, being warned in a dream, he withdrew to the region of Galilee. There he settled in a town called Nazareth so that what had been spoken through the prophets should be fulfilled:

'He will be called a Nazarene.'

THE SCENES NARRATED in Matthew's infancy stories all have Joseph as the principal character. The two scenes which make up this gospel reading are each concluded with a fulfilment citation, one from the prophet Hosea, and the second, 'He will be called a Nazarene', of uncertain origin. Once again Joseph is the receiver of a divine message brought by an angel, firstly to flee to Egypt to avoid Herod's massacre of the children, and then, eventually, to return from there. The report of the actual massacre is reserved for the feast of the Holy Innocents. The story here, on the one hand, has Jesus relive the experience of Israel, of descent into Egypt and exodus from there, and, on the other, shows the family living the millennial experience of refugees, as the most vulnerable people are driven from their homes by the threat of violence. The Son of God quickly becomes a victim of oppression and injustice.

What is the purpose of the fulfilment citations in Matthew?
Consider the present significance of the story of the flight into Egypt.

SUNDAY IN THE CHRISTMAS OCTAVE – FEAST OF THE HOLY FAMILY – YEAR B

A reading from the book of Genesis (15:1-6; 21:1-3)

Some time later, the word of the Lord came to Abram in a vision:

'Do not be afraid, Abram!
I am a shield to you,
and will give you a very great reward.'

Abram replied, 'Lord God, what are you giving to me? I go my way childless, and the heir of my house is Eliezer of Damascus.' Abram continued, 'Look, you have given me no offspring, and see, a member of my household will be my heir.' Then the Lord's word came to him saying, 'This man will not be your heir; no, the issue of your own body shall be your heir.' Then taking him outside, he said, 'Look up at the sky and count the stars if you can. Just so will your descendants be,' he told him. Abram put his faith in the Lord and this was reckoned to him as righteousness.

The Lord treated Sarah as he had said, and did what he had promised her. Sarah conceived and bore Abraham a son in his old age, at the time God had promised. Abraham named the son born to him Isaac, the son to whom Sarah had given birth.

THESE TWO SEPARATE short passages from the book of Genesis tell of the promise made to Abram by God, and of the fulfilment of that promise when Sarah gives birth to Isaac. God is described as the 'shield' of Abram. God has already promised him descendants 'like the dust on the ground' (13:16). Now they are to be 'like the stars'. Abram 'put his faith' (*'aman*) in the Lord. The long night of waiting comes to an end with the fulfilment of God's promise. The text stresses that this child was born to Abraham, whose name has been changed, 'in his old age'. Abraham is one hundred years old (21:5). It is also emphasised that the elderly Sarah, who had laughed at the very thought of becoming a mother (18:12), is indeed the mother of Isaac, whose name means 'he laughs'.

Psalm 105 (104) The psalm praises the fidelity of God, who remembers for ever the covenant made to Abraham.

A reading from the letter to the Hebrews (11:8,11-12, 17-19)

In faith Abraham obeyed the call to *set out* for a place which he was to receive as an inheritance, and *he set out* without knowing where he was going.

In faith Sarah also, in spite of being barren and beyond the age of conception, was made able to receive the seed to bear a child, because she believed that he who had made the promise was faithful. Because of this, from one man, and him as good as dead, were born descendants *as numerous as the stars of heaven and the grains of sand on the seashore which cannot be counted.*

By faith Abraham, *when put to the test, offered up Isaac.* Although he was waiting to receive the promise he was prepared to sacrifice his only son, of whom he had been told: through *Isaac will your name be carried on*. He reckoned that God had the power even to raise the dead, and from there, figuratively speaking, he did receive Isaac back.

THESE VERSES FROM the letter to the Hebrews focus on the faith of Abraham and of Sarah. Abraham, through his faith, as repeatedly affirmed in the book of Genesis, is to receive both a land and numerous descendants. He trusts God to lead him to a new land. He trusts God who promises children as many 'as the stars of heaven and the grains of sand on the seashore'. His trust in God will also involve trial, but God strengthens him to be ready to sacrifice the son of the promise, knowing that God had 'the power to raise the dead'.

A reading from the holy gospel according to Luke (2:22-40)

And when the days were complete for them to be purified in keeping with the Law of Moses, they took him up to Jerusalem to present him to the Lord – as it is written in the Law of the Lord: *Every first-born male shall be called holy to the Lord* – and also to offer in sacrifice, in accordance with what is prescribed in the Law of the Lord, *a pair of turtledoves or two young pigeons*. Now in Jerusalem there was a man named Simeon. He was a righteous and devout man, looking forward to the consolation of Israel, and the Holy Spirit rested on him. It had been revealed to him by the Holy Spirit that he would not see death until he had seen the Christ of the Lord. Prompted by the Spirit he came into the Temple; and when the parents brought in the child Jesus to do for him what the Law required, Simeon himself took him into his arms and blessed God and said:

Now, Master, you are letting your servant
go in peace according to your word;
for my eyes have seen your salvation
which you have made ready in the presence of all nations;
a light for revelation to the gentiles
and for the glory of your people Israel.

As the child's father and mother were wondering at the things that were being said about him, Simeon blessed them and said to Mary his mother, 'Look, he is destined for the fall and for the rise of many in Israel, destined to be a sign that is opposed – and a sword will pierce your soul too – so that the thoughts of many may be laid bare.'

There was a prophetess, too, Anna the daughter of Phanuel, of the tribe of Asher. She was advanced in years, having lived with her husband seven years after her marriage, then as a widow to the age of eighty-four. She never left the Temple, worshipping night and day with fasting and prayer. She came up just at that moment and began to praise God; and to speak about the child to all who looked forward to the deliverance of Jerusalem.

When they had completed everything according to the Law of the Lord, they went back to Galilee, to their own town of Nazareth. And the child grew and became strong, filled with wisdom, and God's favour was on him.

TWO PROPHETS, SIMEON and Anna, welcome the child in the temple of the Lord. Simeon, who has longed for this day, knows that this child is 'a light (*phos*) for the gentiles' and 'the glory (*doxa*) of his people', so that he is now ready to be 'let go in peace'. The widow Anna will continue to speak about the child to all who await 'the deliverance' (*lutrosis*) of Jerusalem. Their faith reflects that of Sarah and Abraham, for they are willing to wait long for God's fulfilment. Mary and Joseph comply with the practices of faith by bringing the child as an offering to God, and Mary is warned of the sword of suffering which will come to her. As Abraham faced the trial of offering his son to God, so Mary and Joseph are ready to follow the paths God will show them.

How are Mary and Joseph examples of faith to inspire us?
Families are nurtured by joy to face the trials ahead.

SUNDAY IN THE CHRISTMAS OCTAVE – FEAST OF THE HOLY FAMILY – YEAR C

A reading from the first book of Samuel (1:20-22, 24-28)

Hannah conceived and, in due course, gave birth to a son, whom she named Samuel, because 'I asked for him from the Lord.' The man Elkanah went up with all his family to offer the annual sacrifice to the Lord and to fulfil his vow. But Hannah did not go, for she had said to

her husband, 'As soon as the child has been weaned I shall bring him and he will appear before the Lord and stay there for ever.'
When she had weaned him, she took him up with her, as well as a three-year-old bull, an *ephah* of flour and a skin of wine, and took him into the temple of the Lord at Shiloh; the child was very young. They sacrificed the bull and led the child to Eli. She said, 'If you please, my lord! As you live, my lord, I am the woman who stood beside you here, praying to the Lord. This is the child for which I was praying, and the Lord has granted me what I asked of him. Now I make him over to the Lord. For the whole of his life he is made over to the Lord.' Then they worshipped the Lord there.

ELKANAH HAD TWO wives. Peninah had children, but Hannah had none, and was mocked by Peninah. Having waited so long for an answer to her prayer, finally Hannah conceives and Samuel is born. It is extraordinary that Hannah is ready to offer her 'very young' child to the Lord for ever. In her gratitude she considers the gift received as a gift to be given back to the Lord. She leaves him with the priest Eli at Shiloh so that he can serve the Lord 'for the whole of his life'. It is as if she knows that the Lord has a mission for this longed-for son, who will be the final judge of Israel and anoint both Saul and David as kings.

Psalm 84 (83) proclaims the happiness of those who dwell in the Lord's house.

A reading from the first letter of St John (3:1-2, 21-24)

See what great love the Father has lavished on us
by letting us be called God's children,
and that is what we are!
The reason why the world does not know us
is that it did not know him.
My dear friends, we are already God's children,
but what we shall be has not yet been revealed.
We know that when he appears

we shall be like him,
for we shall see him as he is.
My dear friends,
if our own hearts do not condemn us,
we can be fearless before God,
and whatever we ask
we shall receive from him,
because we keep his commandments
and do what is pleasing to him.
His commandment is this,
that we should believe in the name of his Son Jesus Christ
and that we should love one another
as he commanded us.
Whoever keeps his commandments
abides in God, and God in that person.
And by this we know that he abides in us,
by the Spirit that he has given us.

THE READING BRINGS together two short sections from the third chapter of the first letter of St John, which consider our identity as 'children of God', and how we should follow his commandments. John addresses Christians as 'my dear friends', or literally 'beloved' (*agapetoi*). Those who believe in Christ are children of God, with the hope of being 'like God', and seeing God as God really is. In the final verses of the chapter, introduced again by 'my dear friends' (*agapetoi*), it is asserted that we can be 'fearless' in the presence of God, asking whatever we wish, because we are members of the family of God and keepers of God's commandments. John explains that the commandment is that we believe 'in the name of his Son Jesus Christ', and that we love one another. This means that we 'abide' (*menein*) in God, and God in us. We know this to be true because we have received the Spirit.

A reading from the holy gospel according to Luke (2:41-52)

Every year the parents of Jesus used to go to Jerusalem for the festival of the Passover. When he was twelve years old, they went up for the festival as usual. When the days of the festival were over and they set off home, the boy Jesus stayed behind in Jerusalem without his parents knowing it. They assumed he was in the party, and after a day's journey they started looking for him among their relations and acquaintances. When they could not find him they went back to Jerusalem looking for him.

It happened that, after three days, they found him in the Temple, sitting among the teachers, listening to them, and asking them questions; and all those who heard him were astounded at his intelligence and his replies. When they saw him they were overcome, and his mother said to him, 'Child, why have you treated us like this? See, your father and I have been searching for you anxiously.' He replied, 'Why were you looking for me? Did you not know that I must be in my Father's house?' But they did not understand what he was saying to them.

He went down with them then and came to Nazareth and lived under their authority. His mother stored up all these things in her heart. And Jesus increased in wisdom, in stature, and in divine and human favour.

THIS GOSPEL STORY is unique in that it is the only account relating to the 'hidden life' of Jesus. The parents of Jesus are once again portrayed as faithful in their observance of Jewish law, going up with the twelve-year old Jesus on the Passover pilgrimage to Jerusalem, just as Elkanah went year by year to the sanctuary of Shiloh. The young Samuel had been deliberately left with Eli, while this story tells, in a way which parents will recognise, that they 'lose' Jesus, who stays behind in the temple. The story suggests that the young Jesus had a consciousness that he should be 'in his Father's house', or involved 'in the things of his Father'. The parents are unable to understand what he means, but, for a second time (2:19), it is stated that Mary pondered 'all these things' (*pemata*) in her heart. This is also the occasion for the evangelist to point to the human growth of Jesus 'in wisdom, in stature, and in divine and human favour'. In reference to John the Baptist the evangelist had spoken of growth 'in spirit' (1:80).

What do these readings teach about the proper attitude of parents to their children?

Jesus was like us in all things but sin, and needed to learn and grow.

26th DECEMBER – FEAST OF ST STEPHEN

A reading from the Acts of the Apostles (6:8-10; 7:54-60)

Stephen, filled with grace and power, began to work great wonders and signs among the people. Then certain people from the synagogue called the Synagogue of Freedmen, and from Cyrene and Alexandria, and others from Cilicia and Asia, came forward to debate with Stephen, but they could not stand up against him because of his wisdom and the Spirit with which he spoke.

When they heard this they were infuriated and ground their teeth at him. But Stephen, filled with the Holy Spirit, gazed into heaven and saw the glory of God and Jesus standing at the right hand of God. He said, 'Look! I see heaven thrown open, and the Son of man standing at the right hand of God.' They cried out in a loud voice and stopped their ears with their hands; then they made a concerted rush at him, thrust him out of the city and began to stone him. The witnesses put down their clothes at the feet of a young man called Saul. As they were stoning him, Stephen said in invocation, 'Lord Jesus, receive my spirit.' Then he knelt down and cried out in a loud voice, 'Lord, do not hold this sin against them.' And with these words he fell asleep.

THE CELEBRATION OF the feast of the first Christian martyr stands in striking contrast to the feast of Christmas. And yet, the Messiah came not for glory but for self-giving. This reading is taken from two chapters of Acts, and the long speech of Stephen to his opponents is omitted. Stephen is full of 'grace' (*charis*) and 'power' (*dunamis*), and works both 'wonders' (*terata*) and 'signs' (*semeia*) for the people. The impact attracts opposition, particularly from Hellenist Jews from various locations, living in Jerusalem. Stephen's very name shows he too was a Hellenist, and he was the first listed among those chosen to serve at tables (6:5). They cannot resist his 'wisdom' (*sophia*) and his 'spirit' (*pneuma*). They are incensed at the fierce tone of his speech (7:1-53). The story of Stephen is modelled by the evangelist on Christ's passion and death. He has a vision of the glory of God and of Jesus at God's right hand (see

Luke 22:69). As they stone him, Stephen offers his life with the words: 'Lord Jesus, receive my spirit.' (see Luke 23:46) He prays: 'Lord, do not hold this sin against them.' (see Luke 23:34) This first martyr witnesses to his Lord not by words alone. Saul stands by. More general persecution will be the aftermath of the stoning of Stephen (8:1).

Psalm 31 (30) The psalm contains repeated words of trust in God.

A reading from the holy gospel according to Matthew (10:17-22)

Jesus said to his disciples: 'Be prepared for people to hand you over to assemblies and scourge you in their synagogues. You will be brought before governors and kings for my sake, as evidence to them and to the gentiles. But when they hand you over, do not worry about how to speak or what to say; what you are to say will be given to you when the time comes, because it is not you who will be speaking; the Spirit of your Father will be speaking in you.

'Brother will betray brother to death, and a father his child; children will come forward against their parents and have them put to death. You will be universally hated on account of my name; but anyone who stands firm to the end will be saved.'

EVEN IN THE Sermon on the Mount Jesus had spoken of persecution in the cause of righteousness (5:10). In the discourse on mission, the second of the five great speeches of Jesus presented by the evangelist Matthew, Jesus speaks more fully about the coming persecution, emphasizing that the 'witness' (*marturion*) will be given not only before Jews but also for the nations. The theme will recur in the final discourse of Jesus concerning the future and the end (24:9). The Spirit of the Father will inspire what the disciples should say in their defence. Jesus himself, when he was interrogated, either remained silent or simply spoke the truth. Betrayal will even come from a person's own family. Hatred will be universal. But anyone who 'stands firm' (*hupomenein*) to the end will attain salvation. Stephen, the first martyr, gives a fine example.

How can the Christmas feast give courage to those suffering the violence of persecution?
The words of Jesus in the gospel are fulfilled in the life of Stephen.

27th DECEMBER – FEAST OF ST JOHN

A reading from the first letter of St John (1:1-4)

What was from the beginning,
what we have heard,
what we have seen with our own eyes,
what we have watched
and touched with our own hands,
about the Word of life,
this is our theme.
This life was revealed;
we have seen it and give testimony,
and declare to you the eternal life,
which was with the Father and was revealed to us.
We are declaring to you
what we have seen and heard,
so that you too may share our life.
Our life is shared with the Father
and with his Son Jesus Christ.
We are writing this to you so that our joy may be complete.

THE FEAST OF St John gently reintroduces us to the Christmas theme. The opening verses of the first letter of John reflect the first verses of the Gospel of John. Both documents speak of the 'Word' *(logos)* that was from the 'beginning' (*arche)*. The first letter of John is a meditative homily which serves as a backdrop to the whole of the season of Christmas. The 'Word of life' (*zoe*) has been revealed (*phaneroun*), and has been heard, seen, watched and touched. This Word, 'which was with the Father', is now proclaimed and creates 'community' (*koinonia*) with the Father and with the Son. This is surely the deepest sense of Christmas, and it gives rise to joy' (*chara*).

Psalm 97 (96) All peoples have seen the glory of the Lord of all the earth, which brings light and joy.

A reading from the holy gospel according to John (20:2-8)

On the first day of the week Mary of Magdala came running to Simon Peter and the other disciple, the one whom Jesus loved, and said to them, 'They have taken the Lord out of the tomb, and we do not know where they have put him.'

So Peter set out with the other disciple to go to the tomb. The two ran together, but the other disciple, running faster than Peter, reached the tomb first; he bent down and saw the linen cloths lying there, but did not go in. Simon Peter, following him, also came up, went into the tomb, saw the linen cloths lying there and also the cloth that had been on his head; this was not with the linen cloths but rolled up in a place by itself. Then the other disciple who had reached the tomb first also went in; he saw and he believed.

MARY OF MAGDALA has brought the message of the empty tomb, but the focus of today's gospel reading is on Peter and 'the disciple Jesus loved', traditionally understood to be the apostle John. At the supper this disciple had been the one reclining next to Jesus (13:23). The one driven by love runs faster and reaches the tomb first. He 'sees' (*blepei*) the linen cloths but does not enter. Apparently acknowledging the leadership of Peter, the beloved disciple allows Peter to enter first into the tomb where Jesus had been laid. Peter 'sees' (*theorei*) the burial cloths, and notes them in detail. The beloved disciple, by contrast, driven by love, 'saw' (*eiden*) and also believed (*pisteuein*). It is difficult to reflect the variety of Greek words involved in the different stages of 'seeing'. When the eyes of love see, they are drawn to faith.

What does the beloved disciple teach us?
Seeing is a stage on the way.

28th DECEMBER – FEAST OF THE HOLY INNOCENTS

A reading from the first letter of St John (1:5-2:2)

This is the declaration we have heard from him
and are declaring to you:
God is light, and there is no darkness in him at all.
If we say that we have fellowship with him
while we are living in darkness,
we are lying, because we are not living the truth.
But if we live in light,
as he is in light,
we have fellowship with one another
and the blood of Jesus, his Son,
cleanses us from all sin.
If we say, 'We have no sin,'
we are deceiving ourselves,
and truth is not in us.
If we acknowledge our sins,
he is trustworthy and righteous
so that he will forgive our sins
and will cleanse us from all evil.
If we say, 'We have never sinned,'
we make him a liar,
and his Word is not in us.
My children, I am writing this so that you do not sin;
but if anyone does sin,
we have an advocate with the Father,
Jesus Christ, the righteous.
He is the sacrifice to expiate our sins,
and not only ours,
but also those of the whole world.

THE PROLOGUE OF the gospel has already spoken of the Word as 'the true light' (John1:5). The first letter goes further and declares that 'God is light' (*phos*), and with him there is no 'darkness' (*skotia*). Believers can still live in darkness, but by acknowledging sin forgiveness is made possible from the one who is 'trustworthy' (*pistos*) and 'just' (*dikaios*). John addresses his readers for the first time as 'children' (*teknia*), and explains that Jesus Christ, who is described as our defender or 'advocate' (*parakletos*), is a 'sacrifice of expiation' (*hilasmos*) for our sins and for those of the whole world. As stated earlier in the passage, 'the blood of Jesus cleanses us' from sin.

Psalm 124 (123) The image of the bird escaping from the 'snare of the fowler' recalls the freedom brought to Christians through the incarnation.

A reading from the holy gospel according to Matthew (2:13-18)

After the wise men had left, see, an angel of the Lord appeared to Joseph in a dream and said, 'Get up. Take the child and his mother, flee into Egypt and stay there until I tell you, for Herod intends to search for the child to destroy him.' So Joseph got up and, taking the child and his mother by night, left for Egypt and stayed there until the death of Herod. This was to fulfil what had been spoken by the Lord through the prophet, saying:

I called my son out of Egypt.

Then Herod, seeing that he had been fooled by the wise men, was furious, and sent and killed in Bethlehem and its surrounding district all the male children who were two years old or less, according to the time he had been careful to ask the wise men. Then was fulfilled what had been spoken through the prophet Jeremiah:

A voice was heard in Ramah,
lamenting and much *weeping,*
Rachel weeping for her children,
and she would not be comforted
because they are no more.

TWO SCENES FROM Matthew's infancy narrative provide the story of the flight into Egypt and the massacre of the male children of Bethlehem. Joseph is again the focus of attention and in a second dream is told to take 'the child and his mother' to Egypt. Joseph is once again willing to respond even 'by night' to the Lord's command. Matthew uses Hosea 11 as a fulfilment citation to conclude this section of the story. The massacre commanded by king Herod would be in keeping with what is known of the historical Herod, king of the Jews, but Matthew may well be drawing a parallel between the situation of the child Jesus and of the child Moses who escapes the slaughter ordered by the Pharaoh in Exodus 1. Matthew uses Jeremiah 31, 'Rachel weeping for her children', to evoke the grief of mothers, and once more to demonstrate that, in the events of the Messiah, Scripture is fulfilled.

Why does Jesus share the experience of his people?
Pray for all victims of massacres, especially the old and the very young.

29th DECEMBER

A reading from the first letter of St John (2:3-11)

In this way we know
that we have come to know him,
if we keep his commandments.
Whoever says, 'I know him'
and does not keep his commandments
is a liar,
and truth has no place in him.
But anyone who does keep his word,
in such a one God's love has truly reached perfection.
By this we know
that we are in God.
Whoever claims to remain in him
must act as he acted.
My dear friends,
this is not a new commandment I am writing for you,

but an old commandment
that you have had from the beginning;
the old commandment is the word you have heard.
Yet in another way,
I am writing a new commandment for you –
and this is true for him and for you –
since darkness is passing away
and the true light is already shining.
Whoever claims to be in light
but hates a brother or sister
is still in darkness.
Whoever loves a brother or sister remains in the light
and has nothing to cause a stumble.
But whoever hates a brother or sister is in darkness
and is walking about in darkness
not knowing the way to go,
because the darkness has brought blindness.

KNOWLEDGE OF JESUS Christ is demonstrated by living his commandments. Through keeping his 'word' (*logos*), the 'love' (*agape*) of God reaches perfection in the person. One who claims to 'remain' (*menein*) in him must imitate him, acting 'as he acted', must 'walk' (*peripatein*) as he walked. For the first time in the letter John addresses his hearers as 'beloved' (*agapetoi*), as 'dear friends', for he is about to speak of a special commandment. It is not 'new' (*kaine*) but 'old' (*palaia*). Yet it has become new, because the darkness is being banished by the 'true light'. Love of the brothers and sisters shows one is living in the light. There is no 'scandal' (*skandalon*), no cause for others to stumble, in a person who loves brothers and sisters. But the one who hates is lost in the darkness, for 'the darkness has blinded his eyes'.

Psalm 96 (95) proclaims a new song for the God who works wonders among all the peoples.

A reading from the holy gospel according to Luke (2:22-35)

And when the days were complete for them to be purified in keeping with the Law of Moses, they took him up to Jerusalem to present him to the Lord – as it is written in the Law of the Lord: *Every first-born male shall be called holy to the Lord* and also to offer in sacrifice, in accordance with what is prescribed in the Law of the Lord, *a pair of turtledoves or two young pigeons.* Now in Jerusalem there was a man named Simeon. He was a righteous and devout man, looking forward to the consolation of Israel, and the Holy Spirit rested on him. It had been revealed to him by the Holy Spirit that he would not see death until he had seen the Christ of the Lord. Prompted by the Spirit he came into the Temple; and when the parents brought in the child Jesus to do for him what the Law required, Simeon himself took him into his arms and blessed God and said:

Now, Master, you are letting your servant
go in peace according to your word;
for my eyes have seen your salvation
which you have made ready in the presence of all nations;
a light for revelation to the gentiles
and for the glory of your people Israel.

As the child's father and mother were wondering at the things that were being said about him, Simeon blessed them and said to Mary his mother, 'Look, he is destined for the fall and for the rise of many in Israel, destined to be a sign that is opposed – and a sword will pierce your soul too – so that the thoughts of many may be laid bare.'

GOING UP TO Jerusalem to observe the requirements of their faith, Mary and Joseph, with their child Jesus, are rewarded by an encounter with the 'man named Simeon', who is described as 'just' (*dikaios*) and 'devout' (*eulabes*), and as one who awaited the 'consolation' (*paraklesis*) of Israel. The holy Spirit, who inspires him, is mentioned three times in three verses. Simeon stands at the end of the line of those who longed to 'see what you see' and to 'hear what you hear' (10:24). The 'salvation' (*soterion*) which he now sees is prepared 'in the presence of all nations'. This Jewish holy man can see beyond the confines of his nation, describing the child he embraces as 'a light (*phos*) for revelation to the gentiles', and 'for the glory (*doxa*) of your people Israel'. Simeon blesses 'his father and mother', speaks of the child as 'a sign that is opposed', and foresees that 'a sword' will pierce Mary's soul.

How does Simeon come to recognise the 'Christ of the Lord'?
The coming of Christ 'reveals the thoughts of many'.

30th DECEMBER

A reading from the first letter of St John (2:12-17)

I am writing to you, children,
because your sins are forgiven through his name.
I am writing to you, parents,
because you have come to know the One who has existed since the beginning.
I am writing to you, young people,
because you have overcome the Evil One.
I have written to you, children,
because you have come to know the Father.
I have written to you, parents,
because you have come to know the One who has existed since the beginning.
I have written to you, young people,
because you are strong,
and God's word remains in you,
and you have overcome the Evil One.
Do not love the world or what is in the world.
If anyone does love the world,
the love of the Father is not in such a person,
because everything there is in the world –
desire of the flesh, desire of the eyes,
pride in possessions –
is not from the Father
but is from the world,

and the world with its desires is passing away.
But whoever does the will of God
remains for ever.

IN ADDRESSING THE children, the parents, and the young, John has words for all. As children, those who believe have come to know the Father, and the forgiveness of sin. As parents, they have come to know the one who exists. As young people, they have the strength to embrace the word of God and to overcome evil. John's letter is addressed to each one, and to everyone, with repeated words of support. He then speaks of the 'world' (*kosmos*) as opposed to God, and as 'passing away'. Steadfastness is to be found in doing the 'will' (*thelema*) of God.

Psalm 96 (95) The psalm proclaims the kingship of God, who created the world and rules in fairness.

A reading from the holy gospel according to Luke (2:36-40)

There was a prophetess, too, Anna the daughter of Phanuel, of the tribe of Asher. She was advanced in years, having lived with her husband seven years after her marriage, then as a widow to the age of eighty-four. She never left the Temple, worshipping night and day with fasting and prayer. She came up just at that moment and began to praise God; and to speak about the child to all who looked forward to the deliverance of Jerusalem.
When they had completed everything according to the Law of the Lord, they went back to Galilee, to their own town of Nazareth. And the child grew and became strong, filled with wisdom, and God's favour was on him.

MARY AND JOSEPH also meet the prophetess Anna. She is eighty-four years old, and never leaves the temple, 'worshipping night and day with fasting and prayer'. Like Simeon, she praises God for the gift of this child. She continues her prophetic role by speaking about him to all who looked forward to the 'deliverance' (*lutrosis*) of Jerusalem. The Messiah comes for the 'consolation' of

Israel, the 'deliverance' of Jerusalem, and stands as a light for all nations. The return to Nazareth allows the evangelist to speak of the growth of Jesus, just as he had spoken of the growth of John (1:80).

What is special about the testimony of Anna?
The voice of the elderly is often a precious gift.

31st DECEMBER

A reading from the first letter of St John (2:18-21)

Children, this is the final hour;
And as you have heard that the Antichrist is coming,
now many Antichrists have already come;
from this we know that it is the final hour.
They have gone from among us,
but they did not belong to us.
If they had belonged to us, they would have stayed with us.
But this was to show
that none of them belonged to us.
But you have been anointed by the Holy One,
and all have knowledge.
I have written to you
not because you do not know the truth,
but because you do know it,
and because no lie comes from the truth.

ONCE AGAIN ADDRESSING the community as 'children' (*paidia*), John speaks of the 'last hour'. It is marked, as expected, by the coming of the 'antichrist' (*antichristos*), or of several antichrists. The word is used only in 1 and 2 John. This is not a reference to 'false Messiahs', as in Mark 13:21-22. It is made clear that these individuals, who were once members of the community, are denying that Jesus is the Christ. They have deserted the community. Those remaining faithful, on the other hand, are reminded that they have, when they became Christians, received an anointing (*chrisma*) from the 'holy one' (*hagios*). They are in possession of the 'truth' (*aletheia*).

> **Psalm 96 (95)** The whole of the cosmos rejoices at the coming of the Lord.

The beginning of the holy gospel according to John (1:1-18)

In the beginning was the Word:
the Word was with God
and the Word was God.
He was with God in the beginning.
Through him all things came into being,
not one thing came into being except through him.
What has come into being in him was life,
life that was the light of all people;
and light shines in darkness,
and darkness could not overpower it.
There was a man sent by God.
His name was John.
He came as a witness,
to bear witness to the light,
so that everyone might believe through him.
He was not the light,
he was to bear witness to the light.
The true light
that gives light to everyone
was coming into the world.
He was in the world
and the world came into being through him,
and the world did not know him.
He came to what was his own
and his own people did not accept him.
But to those who did accept him
he gave power to become children of God,
to those who believed in his name,
who were born not from blood,
or from the will of the flesh,

or from human will
but from God himself.
The Word became flesh,
and lived among us,
and we saw his glory,
the glory as of an only-begotten Son of the Father,
full of grace and truth.
John witnesses to him and cried out, saying,
'This is the one of whom I said:
He who comes after me
has passed ahead of me
because he was before me.'
Indeed, from his fullness
we have all received,
grace upon grace,
for the Law was given through Moses,
grace and truth came through Jesus Christ.
No one has ever seen God;
it is the only-begotten Son,
who is close to the Father's heart,
who has made him known.

ON THE FINAL day of the calendar year, as we approach the end of the octave of Christmas, we hear again the gospel of the Day Mass of Christmas Day. 'The Word (*logos*)', who was 'in the beginning (*arche*)', has been heard as 'truth' (*aletheia*), has been seen as 'light' (*phos*), has been touched as 'flesh' (*sarx*). The Word is full of 'grace' (*charis – hesed*) and 'truth' (*aletheia – 'emet*), the essential qualities of the Father. The Word has given the power to become 'children of God' (*tekna theou*). He has brought 'grace upon grace'. He has 'made known' (*exegeisthai*) the God whom 'no one has ever seen'.

Examine in prayer the central ideas of this passage.
Explore the links between this prologue and the opening verses of 1 John.

1st JANUARY – SOLEMNITY OF MARY MOTHER OF GOD

A reading from the book of Numbers (6:22-27)

The Lord spoke to Moses, saying, 'Speak to Aaron and his sons and say, "This is how you must bless the Israelites. You shall say:

May the Lord bless you and keep you.
May the Lord let his face shine on you and be gracious to you.
May the Lord show you his face and bring you peace.

' "This is how they must call down my name on the Israelites, and I shall bless them." '

THE BLESSING TO be given to the people by Aaron and the priests is punctuated with a triple reference to the divine 'Lord' (*YHWH*). In the first invocation the Lord is asked to 'bless' (*barak*) and 'keep' (*shamar*) them. In Genesis 1 God 'blesses' man and woman, and in Genesis 2 invites them to 'keep' the creation. The second and third invocations ask the Lord, as a sign of favour, to make his 'face' (*panim*) shine upon them, to 'lift up' his 'face' upon them, bringing them 'grace' (*hen*) and 'peace' (*shalom*). We begin the new year with this ancient formula of blessing.

Psalm 67 (66) The psalmist asks God to let his face shine 'upon us'. God's blessing will endure 'till the ends of the earth revere him'.

A reading from the letter of St Paul to the Galatians (4:4-7)

When the fullness of the time came, God sent his Son, born of a woman, born a subject of the Law, to redeem the subjects of the Law, so that we might receive adoption as sons. As you are sons, God has sent into our hearts the Spirit of his Son crying out, '*Abba*, Father'; and so you are no longer a slave, but a son; and if a son, then an heir, made so through God.

THIS UNIQUE ALLUSION to the mother of the Son in Paul's writings underlines once more the full humanity of Jesus, who, in the 'fulness of time' (*to pleroma tou chronou*) was 'born of a woman', and 'born a subject of the Law'. But Paul points us to the new potential for humanity, that human beings are to be 'redeemed', their freedom bought back, so that they are no longer subject to the Law, but rather adopted as children of God. The human birth of the Son from a human mother enables the rebirth of his brothers and sisters as children of God. As sons and daughters we are able to receive the Spirit of the Son in our hearts, which cries out '*Abba Father* with the confidence that our new relationship with the Father gives us, for we are 'slaves no longer but sons and daughters', and 'heirs through God'. The role of Mary was to bestow humanity on the Son, so that he could bestow divinity on his brothers and sisters.

A reading from the holy gospel according to Luke (2:16-21)

The shepherds went in haste and found Mary and Joseph, and the baby lying in the manger. When they saw this, they made known what they had been told about this child, and everyone who heard it was astonished at what the shepherds said to them. But Mary treasured all these things and pondered them in her heart. And the shepherds went back glorifying and praising God for all they had heard and seen, just as they had been told.

When the eight days were complete to circumcise the child, he was called Jesus, the name the angel had given him before he was conceived in the womb.

THE GOSPEL READING spans the octave of Christmas. On Christmas night the shepherds, as they had been told, went to visit the new-born child, and announced to all the astonishing birth. Mary however is silent, simply keeping 'all these things' (*pemata*) in her heart. At the end of the octave, on the eighth day, Jesus is circumcised according to Jewish custom, and named *yeshua*', as had been commanded by the angel to Mary and to Joseph, for he is the one who is to 'save' his people (Luke 1:31 Matthew 1:21).

Why was Jesus circumcised?
Mary suggests that our human response to Christ should be silence.

SECOND SUNDAY AFTER CHRISTMAS

A reading from the book of Ecclesiasticus (24:1-2, 8-12)

Wisdom speaks her own praises,
in the midst of her people she glories in herself.
She opens her mouth in the assembly of the Most High,
in the presence of the Mighty One she glories in herself:
Then the Creator of all things instructed me
and he who created me fixed a place for my tent.
He said, "Pitch your tent in Jacob,
make Israel your inheritance."
Before the ages, in the beginning, he created me
and till eternity I shall remain.
In the holy tent I ministered before him
and thus became established in Zion.
In the beloved city he has given me rest
and in Jerusalem I wield my authority.
I have taken root in an honoured people,
in the Lord's property, in his inheritance.

IN THE WISDOM writings we frequently find the 'Wisdom' (*hokmah – sophia*) which comes from God personified. Here in chapter 24 of the Wisdom of Ben Sira, also known as 'Ecclesiasticus', Wisdom 'speaks her own praises'. She is told to dwell in 'Jacob', among the tribes of Israel. She is described as 'created in the beginning' and 'resting' in the 'beloved city'. The strongest parallel with the incarnation of the Word comes in the command: 'Pitch your tent in Jacob'. John 1:14 reads: 'the Word lived (*eskenesen*) among us', or, more literally, 'pitched his tent with us'. The Word of God is indeed the Wisdom of God.

Psalm 147 (146) God 'sends out his word to the earth'.

A reading from the letter of St Paul to the Ephesians (1:3-6, 15-18)

Blessed be the God and Father of our Lord Jesus Christ,
who has blessed us with every spiritual blessing of heaven in Christ,
as he chose us in Christ before the foundation of the world
to be holy and faultless before him in love,
marking us out beforehand for adoption as sons, through Jesus Christ
according to the generosity of his will;
to the praise of the glory of his grace,
which he lavished on us in the Beloved.

That is why I, having once heard about your faith in the Lord Jesus and your love for all the saints, do not cease to thank God for you, as I remember you in my prayers; that the God of our Lord Jesus Christ, the Father of glory, may give you a spirit of wisdom and revelation in further knowledge of him; that the eyes of your mind may be enlightened for you to see what the hope of his call is, what are the riches of the glory of his inheritance in the saints.

THE LETTER TO the Christians of Ephesus begins with a hymn of praise for the plan of God, who chose us 'from the foundation of the world' to be his adopted children through the abundance of grace (*charis*) lavished on us in Christ. In later verses from the same chapter, Paul prays for the Christians of Ephesus, that their faith may grow, and that 'the God of our Lord Jesus Christ, the Father of glory' may bestow on them a 'spirit of wisdom' (*pneuma sophias*) and of 'revelation' (*apokalupsis*). Paul prays that their eyes be enlightened to be able to see the 'hope of his call' (*elpis tes kleseos autou*), and the 'richness of the glory' *(ploutos tes doxes)* which the saints (*hagioi*) inherit with Christ.

The beginning of the holy gospel according to John (1:1-18)

In the beginning was the Word:
the Word was with God
and the Word was God.
He was with God in the beginning.
Through him all things came into being,
not one thing came into being except through him.

What has come into being in him was life,
life that was the light of all people;
and light shines in darkness,
and darkness could not overpower it.
There was a man sent by God.
His name was John.
He came as a witness,
to bear witness to the light,
so that everyone might believe through him.
He was not the light,
he was to bear witness to the light.
The true light
that gives light to everyone
was coming into the world.
He was in the world
and the world came into being through him,
and the world did not know him.
He came to what was his own
and his own people did not accept him.
But to those who did accept him
he gave power to become children of God,
to those who believed in his name,
who were born not from blood,
or from the will of the flesh,
or from human will
but from God himself.
The Word became flesh,
and lived among us,
and we saw his glory,
the glory as of an only-begotten Son of the Father,
full of grace and truth.
John witnesses to him and cried out, saying,
'This is the one of whom I said:
He who comes after me
has passed ahead of me
because he was before me.'
Indeed, from his fullness

we have all received,
grace upon grace,
for the Law was given through Moses,
grace and truth came through Jesus Christ.
No one has ever seen God;
it is the only-begotten Son,
who is close to the Father's heart,
who has made him known.

AS WISDOM DWELT among the Israelites, so the Word of God, who was with the Father in the beginning (*arche*), makes his tent among us. The coming of the Word transforms human existence, assuring men and women of their destiny as 'children of God' (*tekna theou*). The Law (*nomos*) which was 'given through Moses' was the Wisdom which dwelt in Israel (Ecclesiasticus 24:23), but, in accordance with God's plan, Jesus Christ has brought 'grace' (*charis*) and 'truth' (*aletheia*), the ultimate gifts of the Father. 'No one has seen God', but the 'only-begotten Son' has 'made him known', 'explained him' and 'become his interpreter' (*exegeisthai*).

Where does God dwell today among people?
Consider the stages of God's wonderful plan for our well-being.

2nd JANUARY

A reading from the first letter of St John (2:22-28)

Who is the liar,
but the one who claims that Jesus is not the Christ?
This is the Antichrist,
who denies both the Father and the Son.
No one who denies the Son has the Father.
Anyone who acknowledges the Son has the Father too.
Let what you have heard from the beginning abide in you;
If what you have heard from the beginning abides in you,
you abide in the Son
and in the Father.

And the promise he himself made you
is eternal life.
So much have I written to you
about those who are leading you astray.
But as for you, the anointing you received from him
abides in you,
and you do not need anyone to teach you.
Since the anointing he gave you teaches you everything,
and since it is true, not false,
abide in him just as he taught you.
Therefore abide in him now, children,
so that when he appears we may have confidence
and not shrink from him in shame
at his coming.

JOHN, HAVING SPOKEN about the 'antichrist', indeed several 'antichrists' (2:18), now calls the antichrist the 'liar' (*pseustes*). This is the person who is in denial, who denies that 'Jesus is the Christ'. The thrust of John's gospel was that 'Jesus is the Christ, the Son of God' (20:31) and that such faith leads to life. The antichrist denies both the Father and the Son. In believers, by contrast, what was preached 'from the beginning' should 'abide' (*menein*), for they have received the promise of eternal life. Their 'anointing' (*chrisma*) 'abides' with them. The word 'abide' occurs many times. They are urged not to be led astray but to remain faithful and have 'confidence' (*parresia*) at Christ's 'coming' (*parousia*).

Psalm 98 (97) As with psalm 96, sung two days ago, a 'new song' (*shir hadash*) is ready to be sung.

A reading from the holy gospel according to John (1:19-28)

This is the witness of John, when the Jews sent to him priests and Levites from Jerusalem to ask him, 'Who are you?' He declared, he did not deny but declared, 'I am not the Messiah.' So they asked, 'What then? Are you Elijah?' He replied, 'I am not.' 'Are you the Prophet?' He answered, 'No.' So they said to him, 'Who are you? So that we may give an answer to those who sent us. What do you say about yourself?' So he said, 'I am, as Isaiah prophesied:

A voice of one that cries in the desert:
prepare a way for the Lord.'

Now they had been sent from the Pharisees, and they put a question to him and said, 'Why then are you baptising if you are not the Messiah nor Elijah nor the Prophet?' John answered them, 'I baptise with water; but among you is standing one whom you do not know, the one who is coming after me; and I am not worthy to undo the strap of his sandal.' This happened at Bethany, on the far side of the Jordan, where John was baptising.

JOHN, PRESENTED AS a 'witness' in the earlier verses of the gospel (1:15), now speaks up to the delegation of priests and Levites sent from Jerusalem. He admits to being, in the words of the prophet, 'a voice (*phone*) that cries in the desert'. The fourth gospel takes up the image from Isaiah 40 used by all the gospels (Matthew 3, Mark 1, Luke 3). John testifies further regarding his baptism with water, and announces the coming of another, whose sandal he is unworthy to untie. The scene is being set for his imminent meeting with Jesus 'the next day' (1:29).

Why do the Jerusalem authorities show interest in John?
The priests and Levites are gone before Jesus arrives on the scene.

3rd JANUARY

A reading from the first letter of St John (2:29-3:6)

If you know that God is righteous
you must recognise that everyone who acts righteously
is a child of his.
See what great love the Father has lavished on us
by letting us be called God's children,
and that is what we are!

The reason why the world does not know us
is that it did not know him.
My dear friends, we are already God's children,
but what we shall be has not yet been revealed.
We know that when he appears
we shall be like him,
for we shall see him as he is.
Whoever treasures this hope of him
purifies himself, just as he is pure.
Whoever sins, acts wickedly,
because all sin is wickedness.
And you know that he was revealed in order to take sins away,
and that in him there is no sin.
No one who abides in him sins,
and whoever sins
has neither seen him nor recognised him.

WHAT DOES IT mean to be 'children of God' (*tekna theou*)? The child of God is not recognised by the world. The child of God does not yet know what lies in the future, except that 'we shall be like him' and 'see him as he is'. The child of God thus lives in hope, purifies himself, and knows that 'no one who abides (*menein*) in him sins'. The theme of 'sin' (*hamartia*) will be taken up next.

Psalm 98 (97) The 'new song' is sung by the whole earth.

A reading from the holy gospel according to John (1:29-34)

The next day, John the Baptist saw Jesus coming towards him and said, 'Look, there is the lamb of God that takes away the sin of the world. This is he of whom I said, "After me comes one who has passed ahead of me because he was before me." I did not know him myself, yet I came baptising with water so that he might be revealed to Israel.' And John bore witness, 'I have seen the Spirit come down on him like a dove from heaven and it rested on him. I did not know him myself, but he who sent me to baptise with water said to me, "The man on whom you see the Spirit come down and rest is the one who baptises with the Holy Spirit." I have seen and borne witness that he is the Son of God.'

THIS PART OF the first chapter of the Gospel of John chronicles a series of days. This passage, with the words 'the next day', marks the second day of a week of revelation. John heralds Jesus with the title 'lamb of God' (*ho amnos tou theou*), and states that he 'takes away the sin of the world'. The inspiration seems to come from the Servant Song in Isaiah 53. The Lord has 'laid upon him the iniquity of us all'. He is 'like a lamb led to the slaughterhouse'. John also testifies to seeing 'the Spirit' descend on Jesus (Isaiah 42), and asserts that he 'baptises with the holy Spirit'. John bears witness that Jesus is 'the Son of God'.

Is there also an allusion to the Passover lamb (Exodus 12) here? Explore the Servant songs in Isaiah 42 and Isaiah 52-53.

4th JANUARY

A reading from the first letter of St John (3:7-10)

Children, do not let anyone lead you astray.
Whoever acts righteously is righteous,
just as he is righteous.
Whoever lives sinfully is from the devil,
since the devil has been a sinner from the beginning.
This was the purpose of the revealing of the Son of God,
to undo the work of the devil.
No one who is a child of God sins,
because God's seed remains in him.
Nor can he sin, because he is a child of God.
This is what distinguishes
the children of God from the children of the devil:
no one who fails to live righteously
and fails to love brothers and sisters
is from God.

THE ONE WHO acts 'justly', who 'does 'justice' (*dikaiosune*), is just, as the Lord himself is just. Our translation uses the archaic term 'righteous'. There is a strong contrast between the 'children' who 'do justice' (*poiein dikaiosunen*), and those who 'live sinfully' (*poiein hamartian*). These latter are 'from the devil (*diabolos*)', who 'was a sinner from the beginning'. The allusion is to Genesis 3 and the power to deceive of the serpent. The Son has been 'revealed' (*phaneroun*) to bring release from the works of the devil. Those 'born of God' do not sin, act in justice, and love their brothers and sisters. The new theme of brotherly love is being prepared.

Psalm 98 (97) A 'new song' (*shir hadash*) is sung once again.

A reading from the holy gospel according to John (1:35-42)

The next day John was again standing there with two of his disciples, and looking at Jesus walking by he said, 'Look, there is the lamb of God.' And the two disciples heard him speaking and followed Jesus. Jesus turned round, and seeing them following said, 'What are you looking for?' They answered, 'Rabbi,' – which translated means Teacher – 'where are you staying?' He said to them, 'Come and see'; so they went and saw where he was staying, and stayed with him that day. It was mid-afternoon. One of these two who had heard John speak and had followed him was Andrew, the brother of Simon Peter. He first found his brother Simon and said to him, 'We have found the Messiah' – which is translated Christ – and he took Simon to Jesus. Jesus looked at him and said, 'You are Simon, son of John; you shall be called Cephas' – which means Rock.

THE FOLLOWING DAY John is with two of his disciples and once again points to Jesus with the words 'Look, there is the lamb of God (*ho amnos tou theou*).' The two immediately follow Jesus and a dialogue begins. Jesus' question 'What are you looking for?' is followed by their addressing him as 'rabbi', which means teacher. They join Jesus 'at about the tenth hour' and remain with him. The named disciple, Andrew, whose companion may perhaps be John, is revered as the *protokletos* ('first called'). He seeks out his brother Simon, and voices his conviction 'we have found the Messiah', and then takes Simon to Jesus. Despite the initiative of Andrew, and his statement of faith, the focus shifts to Simon. His being given by Jesus the Aramaic title 'Cephas', which is rendered by the evangelist with the Greek *Petros* ('Rock'), speaks of his prominence among the disciples of Jesus.

What convinces Andrew he has found the Messiah?
Jesus chooses Peter rather than Andrew.

5th JANUARY

A reading from the first letter of St John (3:11-21)

This is the message
which you heard from the beginning,
that we must love one another,
not be like Cain, who was from the Evil One
and murdered his brother.
And why did he murder his brother?
Because his own actions were evil and his brother's righteous.
Do not be surprised, brothers and sisters,
if the world hates you.
We know that we have passed over from death to life
because we love our brothers and sisters.
Whoever does not love, remains in death.
Anyone who hates brother or sister is a murderer,
and you know that no murderers
have eternal life abiding in them.
By this we know love,
that he laid down his life for our sake,
and we too ought to lay down our lives for our brothers and sisters.
If anyone is well off in worldly possessions
and sees a brother or sister in need
but closes the heart to them,
how can God's love abide in such a person?
Children,

let us love not in word and speech,
but in action and truth.
By this we shall know that we belong to the truth
and it will reassure us in his presence,
even if our own hearts condemn us,
that God is greater than our hearts and knows all things.
My dear friends,
if our own hearts do not condemn us,
we can be fearless before God.

LOVE (*AGAPAN*) OF brothers and sisters is now described as the 'message' (*aggelia*) heard from the beginning of the preaching. It is not a later understanding but central to the gospel. Cain who is 'from the evil one' naturally murders the one who does what is right. Love of brothers and sisters leads to the 'world' (*kosmos*) hating us, but it is a clear sign that 'we have passed over from death to life'. The one who does not love 'remains' (*menein*) in death, and becomes a murderer. We have come to know love (*agape*) since he (*ekeinos*) laid down his life for us, and we should do the same. To cling to possessions is another sign of a lack of love. We should 'belong to the truth (*aletheia*)', which will give us 'reassurance' (*parresia*) as we stand before God.

Psalm 100 (99) The psalm invites 'all the earth' to cry out with joy (*simhah*).

A reading from the holy gospel according to John (1:43-51)

The next day Jesus decided to leave for Galilee; he found Philip and said, 'Follow me.' Philip was from Bethsaida, the same town as Andrew and Peter. Philip found Nathanael and said to him, 'We have found him of whom Moses in the Law and the prophets wrote, Jesus, son of Joseph, from Nazareth.' Nathanael said to him, 'From Nazareth? Can anything good come from Nazareth?' Philip replied, 'Come and see.' When Jesus saw Nathanael coming towards him he said of him, 'Here, truly, is an Israelite in whom there is no deception.' Nathanael asked, 'How do you know me?' Jesus replied, 'Before Philip spoke to you, I saw you under the fig tree.' Nathanael answered him, 'Rabbi, you are Son of God, you are King of Israel.' Jesus replied, 'Do you believe because I said I saw you under the fig tree? You will see greater things than that.' Then he said to him, 'Amen, Amen I say to you, you will see heaven opened and the angels of God ascending and descending upon the Son of man.'

THE LOCATION OF the call of Philip is not clear, since Jesus 'has decided to leave for Galilee', and John the Baptist is mentioned no longer. As Andrew had brought Peter, so now Philip, also from Bethsaida, who has been called by Jesus with the words 'follow me', brings Nathanael into the circle of the followers. Nathanael will be mentioned again at the end of the gospel (21:2), where he is identified as coming from Cana. He has traditionally been identified with Bartholomew. While he is sceptical of a prophet arising from Nazareth, Nathanael becomes enthusiastic and bestows new titles on Jesus: he is 'the Son of God' and 'the king of Israel'. The final words of Jesus concern a larger group: 'you (plural) will see heaven opened'.

Are titles important to Jesus?
A vision of the life beyond is a gift to all.

6th JANUARY – SOLEMNITY OF THE EPIPHANY OF THE LORD

A reading from the prophet Isaiah (60:1-6)

Arise, shine out, for your light has come
and the glory of the Lord has dawned upon you.
Look! Though night still covers the earth
and deep gloom the peoples,
over you the Lord has dawned,
over you his glory can be seen.
Nations will come to your light
and kings to the splendour of your dawn.
Lift up your eyes and look around:
all are assembling and coming to you:

your sons coming from far away
and your daughters held firm on the hip.
At this sight you will grow radiant,
your heart will thrill and dilate,
for the riches of the sea will flow to you,
the wealth of the nations come to you.
Throngs of camels will cover you,
young camels of Midian and Ephah;
everyone in Saba will come,
bringing gold and incense
and proclaiming the praise of the Lord.

THE THIRD PART of the book of Isaiah originates in the time after the exile. This great poem, which builds on the optimism of Second Isaiah, expresses hopes for the future, rejoicing in the salvation brought by God. There are repeated references to the coming of the light, and to the splendour of the dawn, even though 'night' still covers the earth, and 'deep gloom' the peoples. The words seem to be addressed to Sion, restored and resplendent. 'Nations' (*goyim)* and 'kings' (*melakim*) are attracted by her glorious light. It is first of all the exiled 'sons' and 'daughters' who return, but the nations follow, drawn to the holy city as they were in the foundational poem of Isaiah 2: 'Come, let us go up to the mountain of the Lord.' The prophet's imagination envisages the coming of 'throngs of camels'. From Midian and Ephah, nearby lands, they come, but also, from the far south, 'everyone in Saba' comes. Their gifts, gold and incense, are worthy of the Lord.

Psalm 72 (71) The Messiah brings justice and establishes peace, attracting the tribute of Tarshish, and the gifts of Sheba and Saba.

A reading from the letter of St Paul to the Ephesians (3:2-3, 5-6)

You have surely heard the commission of God's grace entrusted to me for your sake; that the mystery was made known to me by a revelation, as I have just written briefly. In former generations it was not made known to humanity as it has now been revealed in the Spirit to his holy apostles and prophets, that the gentiles now have the same inheritance and form the same body and share the same promise in Christ Jesus through the gospel.

IT HAS BEEN the role of Paul to reveal that the Messiah was born not only for his own people, but for the nations too. He speaks of 'the commission of God's grace' (*ten oikonomian tes charitos tou theou*) entrusted to him for the sake of the gentiles. It is a 'mystery' (*musterion*) made known to him by a 'revelation' (*apokalupsis*). Paul is thoroughly convinced of his role as 'apostle of the nations' (Romans 11:13). He explains that gentiles share the 'same inheritance' (*sugkleronoma*) of the Jewish people, are one in the 'same body' (*sussoma*) and have received the 'same promise' (*summetocha tes epaggelias*).

A reading from the holy gospel according to Matthew (2:1-12)

After Jesus had been born at Bethlehem in Judaea during the time of King Herod, suddenly some wise men from the east came to Jerusalem, asking, 'Where is the child born king of the Jews? For we saw his star at its rising and have come to worship him.' When King Herod heard this he was perturbed, and the whole of Jerusalem with him. He called together all the chief priests and the scribes of the people, and enquired of them where the Messiah was to be born. They told him, 'At Bethlehem in Judaea, for this is what was written by the prophet:

> *And you, Bethlehem,*
> *in the land of Judah,*
> *you are by no means the least*
> *among the leaders of Judah,*
> *for from you will come a leader*
> *who will shepherd my people Israel.'*

Then Herod secretly summoned the wise men and made certain from them the exact time when the star had appeared, and sent them on to Bethlehem, saying, 'Go and find out accurately about the child, and when you have found him, report back to me, so that I too may go to worship him.' When they had heard the king, they set out. And see, the star they had seen at its rising went before them until it halted over the place where the child was. Seeing the star, they rejoiced with very great joy, and going into the house they saw the child with Mary, his mother, and falling down they worshipped him. Then, opening their treasure chests, they offered him gifts of gold and frankincense and myrrh. But having been warned in a dream not to go back to Herod, they returned to their own country by a different way.

TO WHAT EXTENT has the story of the magi been inspired by the poem of Third Isaiah and by psalms such as Psalm 72, prayed after the first reading? The infancy gospels of Matthew, which began with the annunciation to Joseph, proceed now with the arrival of the magi. This scene features the quotation from the prophet Micah (5:2) which provides an answer to king Herod about the location of the Messiah's birth. The magi evade the clutches of Herod and in the climax of this scene represent the nations of the earth acknowledging their place among the people saved by the life and death of the Christ. The story illustrates that from the very beginning the Messiah is seen as a threat by the powers of the world but as a gift for those who, like the magi, seek the enlightenment of truth.

What motivates Herod the king? What motivates the magi? Matthew, a Jewish gospel, acclaims the arrival of the nations from the very start.

7th JANUARY OR MONDAY AFTER THE EPIPHANY

A reading from the first letter of St John (3:22-4:6)

Whatever we ask
we shall receive from him,
because we keep his commandments
and do what is pleasing to him.
His commandment is this,
that we should believe in the name of his Son Jesus Christ
and that we should love one another
as he commanded us.

Whoever keeps his commandments
abides in God, and God in that person.
And by this we know that he abides in us,
by the Spirit that he has given us.
My dear friends,
do not trust every spirit,
but test the spirits to see whether they are from God,
for many false prophets have gone out into the world.
By this you know the spirit of God:
any spirit that acknowledges Jesus Christ has come in the flesh
is from God,
and every spirit which fails to acknowledge Jesus
is not from God,
but this is the spirit of Antichrist,
of whose coming you have heard.
He is already now in the world.
Children, you are from God
and have overcome them,
because the Spirit who is in you
is greater than the spirit who is in the world.
They are from the world;
therefore what they say is from the world,
and the world listens to them.
We are from God;
whoever knows God listens to us;
anyone who is not from God does not listen to us.
This is how we can know
the spirit of truth and the spirit of falsehood.

THE 'COMMANDMENT' HAS two parts: belief in the Son, and love of the brothers and sisters. These themes will be taken up again in what follows. Those who follow the commandments have the Spirit (*pneuma*) within them. The 'spirit' of the world by contrast does not confess that Jesus has come in the flesh. This is the spirit of antichrist mentioned earlier in the letter (2:18 and 22). The 'children' (*teknia*) addressed here are 'from God' and have 'overcome' (*nikan*). 'Whoever knows God listens to us,' the writer says. We are able to distinguish 'the spirit of truth (*aletheia*)' from 'the spirit of falsehood (*plane*)'.

Psalm 2 The Son begotten by God will possess the ends of the earth.

A reading from the holy gospel according to Matthew (4:12-17, 23-25)

Hearing that John had been arrested he withdrew to Galilee, and leaving Nazara he went and settled in Capernaum, beside the lake, on the borders of Zebulun and Naphtali. This was to fulfil what was spoken by the prophet Isaiah:

Land of Zebulun! Land of Naphtali!
Way of the sea beyond Jordan.
Galilee of the nations!
The people that sat in darkness
have seen a great light;
on those who lived in a country and shadow of death
a light has dawned.

From then onwards Jesus began his proclamation with the message, 'Repent, for the kingdom of Heaven is close at hand.'

He went round the whole of Galilee teaching in their synagogues, proclaiming the good news of the kingdom and curing all kinds of disease and illness among the people. His fame spread throughout Syria, and they brought to him all those who were suffering from diseases and painful complaints of one kind or another, the possessed, epileptics, the paralysed, and he cured them. Large crowds followed him, coming from Galilee, the Decapolis, Jerusalem, Judaea and beyond the Jordan.

MATTHEW'S ACCOUNT OF the Galilee ministry of Jesus is introduced with a further fulfilment citation. Isaiah's words about the lands of Zebulun and Naphtali are matched in the geographical note the evangelist gives, as Jesus makes his base in the lake-side town of Capernaum. 'From then on he began (*apo tote erxato*)', says the evangelist with some solemnity. Jesus began to call for repentance (*metanoieite*), and to announce the arrival of the kingdom of heaven (*he basileia ton ouranon*). Omitting the verses which concern the call of the first disciples, the gospel reading passes on to a summary of Jesus' activity, as he is seen 'teaching' (*didaskein*), 'proclaiming' (*kerussein*) and 'curing' (*therapeuein*). There is an extensive list of the sick, and of the locations from which they travelled. The gospel proclaims the arrival of a 'great light' in the lives of ordinary people.

How does this gospel reading deepen our celebration of Christmas and Epiphany?
Jesus' ministry begins far from Jerusalem, the religious centre.

8th JANUARY OR TUESDAY AFTER THE EPIPHANY

A reading from the first letter of St John (4:7-10)

My dear friends,
let us love one other,
since love is from God
and everyone who loves is a child of God and knows God.
No one who fails to love knows God,
because God is love.
In this, the love of God was revealed among us,
that God sent his only Son into the world
that we might have life through him.
Love consists in this:
not that we loved God,
but that he loved us and sent his Son
as an atoning sacrifice for our sins.

THIS PASSAGE RETURNS once more to the theme of love: 'love is from God (*ek tou theou*)', makes Christians 'children of God', and allows us to 'know God'. Indeed, 'God is love (*ho theos agape estin*)'. God's love was made known when God sent the only Son into the world so that we might have life. Love has its origin in God, who sent his Son as 'an atoning sacrifice (*hilasmos*)'. The word *hilasmos* may also be translated as 'expiation'. It is not to be translated 'propitiation', as if God had to be placated by our actions. As in 2:2, where it was translated 'sacrifice to expiate', the word suggests God's way of removing the barrier between God and ourselves erected by our sins. This is brought about by God's love shown in the actions of the Son: 'God loved us and sent his Son as an atoning sacrifice for our sins.'

Psalm 72 (71) The Messiah brings justice and peace.

A reading from the holy gospel according to Mark (6:34-44)

As Jesus stepped ashore he saw a large crowd; and he took pity on them because they were like sheep without a shepherd, and he began to teach them many things. By now it was getting late, and his disciples came up to him and said, 'This is a lonely place and it is getting late; send them away, so that they can go to the farms and villages round about and buy themselves something to eat.' He replied, 'Give them something to eat yourselves.' They answered, 'Are we to go and buy bread for two hundred denarii for them to eat?' He asked, 'How many loaves have you? Go and see.' And when they had found out they said, 'Five, and two fish.' Then he instructed them to get all the people to sit down in groups on the green grass, and they sat down on the ground in groups of hundreds and fifties. Then taking the five loaves and the two fish, and raising his eyes to heaven he blessed and broke the loaves and began handing them to his disciples to distribute among the people. He also shared out the two fish among them all. They all ate as much as they wanted. They took up twelve basketfuls of the broken pieces and of the fish. Those who had eaten the loaves numbered five thousand men.

THIS IS THE first of two accounts of the feeding of the multitude in the Gospel of Mark. In these final days of Christmas it reminds us of Jesus' compassion and his concern for those in need, which are the motivation for his coming. Jesus is compared to the shepherd and his feeding of the crowds is both for heart and body. He taught them 'many things', and followed this by feeding them so that 'all ate as much as they wanted'. The Christmas feasts invite us to appreciate the gift of his coming, and the gifts he continues to bring to nourish our lives.

Does Jesus fulfil the hopes and dreams of the prophets and the psalms? Jesus involves his disciples in feeding the hungry.

9th JANUARY OR WEDNESDAY AFTER THE EPIPHANY

A reading from the first letter of St John (4:11-18)

My dear friends,
if God loved us so much,
we too should love one other.
No one has ever seen God,
if we love one other
God abides in us
and his love comes to perfection in us.
By this we know that we abide in him
and he in us,
because he has given us a share in his Spirit.
We ourselves have seen and testify
that the Father sent his Son
as Saviour of the world.
Anyone who acknowledges that Jesus is the Son of God,
God abides in him and he in God.
And we have come to know
and believe the love God has for us.
God is love,
and whoever abides in love abides in God
and God in him.
Love has come to its perfection in us
so that we may face the Day of Judgement fearlessly,
because as he is,
so are we in this world.
In love there is no fear,
but perfect love drives out fear,
because fear has to do with punishment,
and one who fears has not come to perfection in love.

WE HAVE NEVER seen God, but God dwells in us if we love each other. Furthermore, God has given us 'a share in his Spirit (*ek tou pneumatos*)', which allows us to witness that the Father sent the Son as 'Saviour (*soter*)'. We are fully convinced of the love God has for us. Once again the writer affirms that 'God is love (*ho theos agape estin*)' (4:8 and 4:16). We 'abide' (*menein*) in God, and God in us. God's love allows us to have confidence (*parresia*) in the face of God's judgement, for love casts out fear.

Psalm 72 (71) The Messiah saves the poor and the needy.

A reading from the holy gospel according to Mark (6:45-52)

And at once he made his disciples get into the boat and go on ahead to the other side near Bethsaida, while he himself sent the crowd away. After parting from them he went off to the mountain to pray. When evening came, the boat was far out on the sea, and he was alone on the land. Seeing that they were hard pressed in their rowing, for the wind was against them, not long before dawn he came towards them, walking on the sea. He was going to pass them by, but when they saw him walking on the sea they thought it was a phantom and cried out; for they had all seen him and were terrified. But at once he spoke to them and said, 'Courage! It's me! Don't be afraid.' Then he got into the boat with them and the wind dropped. They were utterly and completely dumbfounded, because they had not understood about the loaves, but their hearts were hardened.

THIS GOSPEL PASSAGE follows directly from the account of the multiplication of the loaves read yesterday. Jesus is the one who feeds the multitude. Jesus is the one who has power over the sea. The evangelist is suggesting that Jesus has powers greater than Moses, to feed the minds and bodies of the people, and to protect them from harm. The disciples were 'completely and utterly dumbfounded', and yet their hearts remained 'hardened'.

What relevance does this gospel passage have to the Christmas feasts?
The graces of Christmas can be met with hardness of heart and slowness of faith.

10th JANUARY OR THURSDAY AFTER THE EPIPHANY

A reading from the first letter of St John (4:19-5:4)

Let us love
because he first loved us.
Anyone who says 'I love God'
and hates a brother or sister
is a liar,
since whoever does not love the brother or sister whom he has seen
cannot love God whom he has not seen.
This is the commandment we have received from him,
that whoever loves God loves also brother and sister.
Whoever believes that Jesus is the Christ
is a child of God,
and whoever loves the father
loves the son.
In this we know that we love God's children,
whenever we love God and keep his commandments,
for this is what the love of God is:
keeping his commandments;
and his commandments are not burdensome,
because whatever is born of God
conquers the world,
and this is the victory that has overcome the world – our faith.

ONCE MORE THE writer states that it is God who is the first to love (4:10, 4:19). Hatred of a brother or sister is incompatible with love of God. The commandment we have received is that those who love God must also love brother and sister. All who believe that Jesus is the Christ are children of God, loving both the Father and the Son. We have won a victory (*nikan*) over the world (*kosmos*) by our faith, a faith lived out in love.

Psalm 72 (71) The Messiah will free the poor from oppression.

A reading from the holy gospel according to Luke (4:14-22)

Jesus returned to Galilee in the power of the Spirit, and his reputation spread throughout the countryside. He kept teaching in their synagogues and was glorified by everyone.

He came to Nazara, where he had been brought up, and went into the synagogue on the Sabbath as was his custom. He stood up to read, and he was given the scroll of the prophet Isaiah. Unrolling the scroll he found the place where it is written:

The spirit of the Lord is upon me,
for he has anointed me to bring good news to the poor.
He has sent me to proclaim release to captives,
sight to the blind, to let the oppressed go free,
to proclaim a year of the Lord's favour.

He then rolled up the scroll, gave it back to the assistant and sat down. And the eyes of all in the synagogue were fixed on him. Then he began to speak to them, 'Today this text has been fulfilled in your hearing.' And all bore witness to him, and were astonished by the words of grace that came from his lips.

THE MINISTRY OF Jesus in the Gospel of Luke, unlike the other gospels, after a short summary statement (4:14-15), begins with the visit to the synagogue in Nazareth. Luke shows Jesus reading from the book of Isaiah and proclaiming a text from the Third Isaiah: 'The spirit of the Lord is upon me.' In this way Luke has Jesus announce his purpose, 'to bring good news to the poor'. This gospel text is very appropriate during the last days of Christmas, as Jesus emerges from ordinary life and takes on his role as a prophet who will face both acclaim and rejection.

Why is preaching in synagogues so important to Jesus?
This account of Jesus in the Nazareth synagogue precedes the calling of the disciples.

11th JANUARY OR FRIDAY AFTER THE EPIPHANY

A reading from the first letter of St John (5:5-13)

Who can overcome the world
but the one who believes that Jesus is the Son of God?
He it is who came by water and blood,
Jesus Christ,
not with water alone
but with water and blood,
and it is the Spirit that bears witness,
for the Spirit is Truth.
So there are three witnesses,
the Spirit, the water and the blood,
and these three are one.
If we accept the testimony of human witnesses,
God's testimony is greater,
for this is God's testimony
which he gave about his Son.
Whoever believes in the Son of God
has this testimony within him,
and whoever does not believe
is making God a liar,
for not believing
the testimony God has given about his Son.
And this is the testimony:
God has given us eternal life,
and this life is in his Son.
Whoever has the Son has life,
and whoever does not have the Son of God does not have life.
I have written this to you
who believe in the name of the Son of God
so that you may know that you have eternal life.

THE WRITER SPEAKS once again about the one who 'has victory' (*nikan*) over the 'world' (*kosmos*). It is the one who believes that Jesus is the Son of God. Jesus came 'by water and blood'. Does the water allude to baptism, even though no baptism of Jesus is recounted in John's gospel? Or is this rather an allusion to the water and blood from the side of Jesus at his death (John 19:34)? John then says that the Spirit (*pneuma*) also bears witness (*marturein*), the spirit of truth, and that there are consequently 'three' who bear witness: the spirit, the water and the blood. The witness, or testimony (*marturia*), ultimately comes from God, and this testimony is that God has given us eternal life in the Son. This is the essential truth of Christmas and of Christianity.

Psalm 147 (146) The Lord has 'sent out his word to the earth'.

A reading from the holy gospel according to Luke (5:12-16)

Now it happened that Jesus was in one of the towns when, suddenly, a man appeared, covered with leprosy. Seeing Jesus he bowed with his face to the ground and implored him saying, 'Lord, if you are willing you can cleanse me.' Jesus stretched out his hand, and touched him saying, 'I am willing. Be cleansed.' At once the leprosy left him. He ordered him to tell no one, 'But go and show yourself to the priest and make the offering for your cleansing just as Moses prescribed, as evidence to them.'

But the news of him spread still more, and large crowds would gather to hear him and to be cured of their illnesses, but he would withdraw to deserted places and pray.

JESUS HEALS A man 'covered with leprosy' (*pleres lepras*). The faith of this man is expressed in his bowing 'with his face to the ground', and in his words of faith, 'Lord, if you are willing, you can cleanse me'. Reading this gospel passage in the final days of Christmas reminds us again that he has come 'to bring good news to the poor', and that no-one is to be excluded, and no-one is beyond the healing compassion of the Messiah. It is not the healed man who spreads the news. The sheer number of people wanting the attention of Jesus does not allow the news to be contained, but Jesus seeks solitude 'in deserted places'.

Why is Jesus reluctant that the news of healing be spread?
Jesus combines pastoral activity and prayer.

12th JANUARY OR SATURDAY AFTER THE EPIPHANY

A reading from the first letter of St John (5:14-21)

This is the fearlessness we have towards him,
that if we ask anything in accordance with his will
he hears us.
And if we know that he listens to whatever we ask him,
we know that we already possess whatever we have asked of him.
Anyone who sees a brother or sister commit a sin
that is not a deadly sin,
has only to pray, and God will give life to this person,
provided that it is not a deadly sin.
There is sin that leads to death
and I am not saying you should pray about that.
Every kind of wickedness is sin,
but not all sin leads to death.
We know that no one who is a child of God sins,
because he who was born from God protects such a one,
and the Evil One cannot touch such a one.
We know that we are from God,
and the whole world lies open to the Evil One.
We know also that the Son of God has come
and has given us understanding
so that we may know him who is true.
We are in the One who is true
in his Son, Jesus Christ.
He is the true God
and eternal life.
Children, be on your guard against idols.

LOVE CASTS OUT fear (4:18), and 'fearlessness (*parresia*)' allows us to make requests of God with total confidence, whatever our needs. We can pray for the forgiveness of sin on behalf of a brother or sister, and life will be restored to that person. But John also speaks about 'sin that leads to death (*hamartia pros thanaton*)', though it is unclear what he means. He is probably alluding to those who deny Jesus is the Son of God, and who have deserted the community (2:18-19, 22). But those 'born of God' do not sin, even though the 'whole world lies open to the Evil One'. The Messiah has come to give us 'understanding' (*dianoia*) so that we may know 'him who is true (*alethinon*)'. We are 'in the One who is true' and 'in his Son, Jesus Christ'. He is the true God and eternal life. The final words of the letter are 'children, be on your guard against idols'.

Psalm 149 Once again we are invited to sing 'a new song (*shir hadash*)' for the gift of salvation.

A reading from the holy gospel according to John (3:22-30)

After this, Jesus and his disciples went into the Judaean countryside and he spent some time with them there and baptised. And John also was baptising at Aenon near Salim, because there was plenty of water there, and people were going there and were being baptised. For John had not yet been thrown into prison. Now a discussion arose between John's disciples and a Jew about purification, so they went to John and said, 'Rabbi, the man who was with you on the far side of the Jordan, to whom you bore witness, is baptising now, and everyone is going to him.' John replied:

'No one can receive anything
except what is given from heaven.
'You yourselves can bear witness to me that I said, "I am not the Messiah;
but I am the one who has been sent ahead of him."
'He who has the bride is the bridegroom,
and yet the bridegroom's friend,
who stands and listens to him,
is filled with joy at the bridegroom's voice.
This joy of mine is complete.
He must grow greater, I must grow less.'

ONLY IN THIS text do we have reference to Jesus baptising. But there is of course no rivalry between them, for John affirms, 'No one can receive anything except what is given from heaven'. John has constantly maintained that his role is to prepare the way. John gives his final testimony about Jesus and refers to himself as 'the friend of the bridegroom' (*ho philos tou numphiou*), who rejoices for his friend. There is a possible allusion here to Isaiah's song of the vineyard, in which the prophet sings for his friend about his love for his vineyard (Isaiah 5:1). The 'joy (*chara*)' of John is now complete as the ministry of Jesus begins. The remarks of John, that Jesus is to grow greater, while he is to grow less, are a further confirmation of his role as deferring to Jesus, and 'preparing the way', found in every gospel. We are reminded that the feast of the birth of John, at the time of the longest day in the northern hemisphere, heralds the time in which the light will 'grow less', while the Christmas feast, at the time of the shortest day, introduces the light of the Messiah which will 'grow greater'. Nature appropriately reflects the births of John and of Jesus.

Why has John the Baptist been so prominent in Advent and Christmas? The end of Christmas shows John's final witness to the one who was to come after him.

FEAST OF THE BAPTISM OF THE LORD – YEAR A

A reading from the prophet Isaiah (42:1-4, 6-7)

Here is my servant whom I uphold,
my chosen one in whom my soul delights.
I have put my spirit upon him,
he will bring fair judgement to the nations.
He will not cry out or raise his voice,
his voice will not be heard in the street.
A crushed reed he will not break
nor will he snuff out a faltering wick.
He will establish fair judgement for the nations.
He will not grow faint or be discouraged

until he has established fair judgement on earth
and the coastlands are waiting for his guidance.
I the Lord have called you in righteousness,
I have grasped you by the hand and watched over you;
I have given you as a covenant for the people
and light for the nations,
to open the eyes of the blind,
to free captives from prison,
and those who sit in darkness from the dungeon.

THE SECOND PART of Isaiah (40-55) contains four 'songs' of the 'suffering servant', read during Holy Week. The first song is also appropriate for this final day of the Christmas season, on which we consider the start of Jesus' ministry with his baptism by John. At the baptism he will be called 'son' and 'beloved'. The names given here, also appropriate, are 'servant (*'ebed*)' and 'chosen one (*bahir*)'. The style of the servant is humble and unthreatening, but he is committed to bringing 'fair judgement (*mishpat*)'. He is a person of integrity and truth. The servant is to be 'light for the nations (*'or goyim*)', bringing sight for the blind and freedom for prisoners. These actions are central to the ministry of Jesus of Nazareth.

Psalm 29 (28) The voice of the Lord resounds over the waters.

A reading from the Acts of the Apostles (10:34-38)

Then Peter began to speak to Cornelius and his household: 'I understand that truly God is impartial, but that in every nation one that fears him and does what is righteous is acceptable to him. You know the message which he sent to the children of Israel proclaiming peace through Jesus Christ – he is Lord of all – the word which spread throughout Judaea, beginning from Galilee after the baptism which John announced: Jesus of Nazareth, whom God anointed with the Holy Spirit and with power, who went around doing good and healing all who were held in the power of the devil, because God was with him.

PETER ANNOUNCES THE good news to Cornelius, the Roman centurion, at his house in Caesarea. Peter realises that the God of Jesus Christ is the God of all people, all those who 'fear' him and do what is just (*dikaiosune*). Jesus' public life had begun after John's baptism. In Peter's words, Jesus was 'anointed' by God with the 'Holy Spirit (*pneuma hagion*)' and with 'power (*dunamis*)'. Peter does not mention his baptism by John explicitly, but simply the descent of the Spirit which is mentioned in the gospel accounts, so that Jesus can begin his work of 'doing good' and 'healing'.

A reading from the holy gospel according to Matthew (3:13-17)

Then Jesus came from Galilee to the Jordan to be baptised by John. John tried to prevent him, saying, 'I need to be baptised by you, and yet do you come to me?' But Jesus replied, 'Leave it for the time being; for so it is fitting that we should fulfil all righteousness.' Then he allowed him. And when Jesus had been baptised he at once came up from the water, and see, the heavens opened and he saw the Spirit of God descending like a dove and coming down on him. And see, a voice from heaven, 'This is my Son, the Beloved, in whom I am well pleased.'

THE UNIQUE FEATURE of Matthew's account of the baptism of Jesus is that John expresses reluctance to baptise him. John feels the need to be baptised by Jesus. But Jesus insists that 'righteousness (*dikaiosune*)' be fulfilled. The one who stands alongside sinners seeking repentance has the humility to undergo the same rite of penance that they perform. In this account, as in Mark's, it is Jesus alone who sees the Spirit of God descending, yet the 'voice (*phone*) from heaven' speaks to all present saying: 'This is my Son, the Beloved, in whom I am well pleased.'

To what extent is Jesus imitating the suffering servant when he goes for baptism?

Consider how each evangelist highlights the presence of the Spirit at the baptism of Jesus.

FEAST OF THE BAPTISM OF THE LORD – YEAR B

A reading from the prophet Isaiah (55:1-11)

'O you who are thirsty, come to the water!
You who have no money, come buy and eat!
Come buy wine and milk without money, free!
Why spend money on what cannot nourish
and your earnings on what fails to satisfy?
Listen carefully to me:
have good things to eat and rich food to enjoy.
Pay attention, come to me; listen, and you will live.
I shall make an everlasting covenant with you –
the mercies of my steadfast love for David.
Look, I have put him as a witness to peoples,
a leader and lawgiver to peoples.
Look, you will summon a nation unknown to you;
nations unknown to you will hurry to you
for the sake of the Lord your God
because the Holy One of Israel has made you glorious.
Seek the Lord while he is to be found,
call to him while he is near.
Let the wicked abandon their ways
and the sinful their thoughts.
Let them turn back to the Lord
that he may have mercy on them,
to our God, for he is rich in forgiveness.
For my thoughts are not your thoughts
and your ways are not my ways – declares the Lord.
For as the heavens are high above earth
so are my ways above your ways,
my thoughts above your thoughts.
For as the rain and the snow come down from the sky
and do not return before watering the earth,
fertilising it and making it germinate
to provide seed for the sower and food to eat,

so it is with the word that goes forth from my mouth:
it does not return to me unfulfilled
or before carrying out my purpose
and achieving what it was sent to do.

THE FINAL CHAPTER of the second part of Isaiah begins with the invitation to come to the water and drink, to come and eat. God's gifts are freely given. 'Listen and you will live!' God reaffirms his 'everlasting covenant (*berit 'olam*)'. It is renewed at the return from exile, and further renewed by Jesus Christ, and by baptism into his new life. On this final day of the Christmas season we are urged to 'seek (*darash*)' the Lord, and to 'call (*qara'*)' on him. God's ways are different and surprising. This is what Christmas has taught. But those who are open to the 'word (*dabar*)' that comes from God, and are 'watered' by his rain, will be given new life by his gifts.

Isaiah 12 This canticle from Isaiah offers the 'water of salvation'.

A reading from the first letter of St John (5:1-9)

Whoever believes that Jesus is the Christ
is a child of God,
and whoever loves the father
loves the son.
In this we know that we love God's children,
whenever we love God and keep his commandments,
for this is what the love of God is:
keeping his commandments;
and his commandments are not burdensome,
because whatever is born of God
conquers the world,
and this is the victory that has overcome the world –
our faith.
Who can overcome the world
but the one who believes that Jesus is the Son of God?
He it is who came by water and blood,
Jesus Christ,

not with water alone
but with water and blood,
and it is the Spirit that bears witness,
for the Spirit is Truth.
So there are three witnesses,
the Spirit, the water and the blood,
and these three are one.
If we accept the testimony of human witnesses,
God's testimony is greater,
for this is God's testimony
which he gave about his Son.

THE CHILDREN OF God know that Jesus is the Christ. They follow God's commandments by loving all God's children. The Son of God came with the 'witness' of water, for he was baptised by John in the Jordan, and with the 'witness' of blood, for he is 'the Lamb who takes away the sins of the world' (John 1:29). The third witness is the Spirit of truth, who gives testimony with the Father at the baptism of Jesus.

A reading from the holy gospel according to Mark (1:7-11)

And as he proclaimed John said, 'After me is coming the one who is more powerful than me, and I am not fit to kneel down and undo the strap of his sandals. I have baptised you with water, but he will baptise you with the Holy Spirit.'

It was in those days that Jesus came from Nazareth in Galilee and was baptised in the Jordan by John. And at once, as he was coming up out of the water, he saw the heavens torn apart and the Spirit, like a dove, descending on him. And a voice came from heaven, 'You are my Son, the Beloved; in you I am well pleased.'

THE FIRST ACTION of Jesus in the Gospel of Mark is to seek baptism from John. The text is unambiguous: 'he was baptised in the Jordan by John'. Baptism for repentance might be considered inappropriate in the case of Jesus, but solidarity with sinners suggests its real purpose. It is Jesus himself who sees 'the heavens torn apart' and 'the Spirit, like a dove, descending'. The voice of the Father affirms approval of the Son, the 'Beloved (*agapetos*)'.

Why does Jesus seek the baptism of John?
Jesus is silent at his baptism in Mark.

FEAST OF THE BAPTISM OF THE LORD – YEAR C

A reading from the prophet Isaiah (40:1-5, 9-11)

'Comfort, O comfort my people,'
says your God.
'Speak to the heart of Jerusalem
and cry out to her
that her period of service is ended,
her penalty has been paid;
from the hand of the Lord she has received
double for all her sins.'
A voice crying out,
'In the desert prepare a way for the Lord.
Make straight across the wastelands
a highway for our God.
Let every ravine be filled in,
every mountain and hill be brought down;
the crooked shall be straight,
the rough places a plain.
Then the glory of the Lord shall be revealed
and all humanity shall see it together,
for the mouth of the Lord has spoken.'
Go up on a high mountain, Zion,
herald of good news!
Lift up your voice with power, Jerusalem,
herald of good news!
Lift it up without fear!
Say to the cities of Judah,
'See, here is your God.'
See the Lord God coming with power,
his arm rules for him,

see, his reward is with him,
his prize goes before him.
He tends his flock like a shepherd,
gathering the lambs in his arms,
holding them against his breast
and leading the mother ewes.

THE OPENING CHAPTER of the second Isaiah, familiar during Advent, is read again on this final day of the Christmas season. It announced to the people: 'See, here is your God.' The faithful God cares for his people and like a shepherd brings them home from exile. The feast of the Baptism of the Lord has the Father announce: 'This is my Son, the beloved!' The fidelity of God is again apparent in the self-offering of Jesus, as he shows solidarity with the people who seek the good news of God's forgiveness.

Psalm 104 (103) This great psalm of creation speaks of the Spirit who brings life.

A reading from the letter of St Paul to Titus (2:11-14, 3:4-7)

The grace of God our Saviour has been revealed to the whole human race, teaching us that, giving up impiety and all worldly passions, we should be self-restrained and live righteous and religious lives in this present world, waiting for the blessed hope and the appearing of the glory of our great God and Saviour Christ Jesus. He offered himself for us in order to ransom us from all our faults and to purify a people to be his very own, eager to do good. When the kindness and love of God our Saviour for humanity were revealed, not because of any works of righteousness we had ourselves done but in accordance with his own mercy, he saved us through the washing of rebirth and renewal in the Holy Spirit which he generously poured over us through Jesus Christ our Saviour so that, justified by his grace, we should become heirs in hope of eternal life.

THE TWO PARTS of this reading served as the second reading at the Night Mass and the Dawn Mass of Christmas Day. They speak of the 'revealing (*epiphaneisthai*)' of the 'grace (*charis*)' of God (2:11), and of the 'kindness (*chrestotes*)' and 'love (*philanthropia*)' of God our Saviour (3:4). These three attributes of God, which are virtually synonymous, are revealed in the gift of the Son. God through Christ 'ransomed (*lutroun*)' us, and 'purified (*katharizein*)' us. God's kindness was not deserved by any 'works of justice (*dikaiosune*)' we have performed, but he saved us 'in accordance with his mercy (*eleos*)', 'through the washing of rebirth (*dia loutrou paliggenesias*)', and through 'the renewal in the Holy Spirit (*anakainoseos pneumatos hagiou*)', doubtless references to the baptism by which Christians are given new life through water and the Holy Spirit.

A reading from the holy gospel according to Luke (3:15-16, 21-22)

There was a feeling of expectancy among the people; they were all questioning in their hearts whether John might himself be the Messiah. John answered them all by saying, 'I baptise you with water, but one more powerful than me is coming, and I am not fit to undo the strap of his sandals; he will baptise you with the Holy Spirit and with fire.'
Now it happened that while all the people were being baptised and while Jesus, after his own baptism, was at prayer, heaven opened and the Holy Spirit descended on him in a physical form, like a dove. And a voice came from heaven, 'You are my Son, the Beloved; in you I am well pleased.'

THIS VERSION OF the baptism of Jesus taken from the gospel of Luke includes a part of the preparatory preaching of John the Baptist, in which he speaks of baptism 'with the Holy Spirit (*pneuma hagion*) and with fire'. The baptism of Jesus is reported rather obliquely because the accent is on the prayer of Jesus, and the manifestation of the Spirit. The voice of God is addressed to Jesus, in words identical with those found in Mark's account (Mark 1:11).

Why does John refer to baptism 'in fire' (Matthew 3:11 Luke 3:16)?
Jesus is frequently found at prayer in the gospel of Luke.